IN THE NAME OF

ALLAH

THE ALL-COMPASSIONATE, ALL-MERCIFUL

«A woman is like a rib which will break if you try to straighten it. You can benefit from it even if it remains bent as it was made.»

(Hadith in *Ṣaḥeeḥ Muslim*, 'The Book of Marriage')

Bent Rib

A Journey through Women's Issues in Islam

- Title: **Bent Rib**: A Journey through Women's Issues in Islam
- Author: Huda Khattab
- New Revised English Edition 3 (2010)
- Layout Design: IIPH, Riyadh, Saudi Arabia
- Filming & Cover Design: Samo Press Group

Bent Rib

A Journey through Women's Issues in Islam

THIRD EDITION

مسائل تهم المرأة في الإسلام

Huda Khattab

الدار العالمية للكتاب الإسلامي

INTERNATIONAL ISLAMIC PUBLISHING HOUSE

Copyright © 2010 International Islamic Publishing House
King Fahd National Library Cataloging-in-Publication Data

Khattab, Huda
    Bent Rib: a journey through women's issues in Islam. /
Huda Khattab 3.- Riyadh, 2010

    176 p ; 21 cm

    ISBN Hardcover: 978-603-501-034-4

    1- Women in Islam   I- Title

    219.1 dc   1431/2122

Legal Deposit no. **1431/2122**
ISBN Hardcover: **978-603-501-034-4**

International Islamic Publishing House (IIPH)
P.O. Box 55195 Riyadh 11534, Saudi Arabia
Tel: 966 1 4650818 / 4647213 — Fax: 966 1 4633489
E-mail: iiph@iiph.com.sa — iiphsa@gmail.com
www.iiph.com.sa

Contents

CHAPTER NINE
Beyond Home Economics:
Education for Girls and Women.....................................135

Pronunciation and Transliteration Chart

Arabic script	Pronunciation	Transliterated as:
أ	short 'a', as in *cat*	a
آ – ى	longer 'a', as in *cab* (not as in *cake*)	â
ب	/b/ as in *bell, rubber* and *tab*	b
ت	/t/ as in *tap, mustard* and *sit*	t
ة	takes the sound of the preceding diactrical mark sometimes ending in h (when in pausal form): ah, ih, or ooh; or atu(n), ati(n) or ata(n) when in uninterrupted speech	h or t (when followed by another Arabic word)
ث	/th/ as in *thing, maths* and *wealth*	th
ج	/j/ as in *jam, ajar* and *age*	j
ح	a 'harsher' sound than the English initial /h/, and may occur medially and in word-final position as well	ḥ
خ	as in *Bach* (in German); may occur initially and medially as well	kh
د	/d/ as in *do, muddy* and *red*	d
ذ	as in *this, father*, and *with*	dh
ر	/r/ as in *raw, art* and *war*; may also be a rolled r, as with Spanish words	r

Arabic script	Pronunciation	Transliterated as:
ز	/z/ as in *zoo*, *easy* and *gaze*	z
س	/s/ as in *so*, *messy* and *grass*	s
ش	as in *ship*, *ashes* and *rush*	sh
ص	no close equivalent in English, but may be approximated by pronouncing it as /sw/ or /s/ farther back in the mouth	ṣ
ض	no close equivalent in English, but may be approximated by pronouncing /d/ farther back in the mouth	ḍ
ط	no close equivalent in English, but may be approximated by pronouncing /t/ farther back in the mouth	ṭ
ظ	no close equivalent in English, but may be approximated by pronouncing 'the' farther back in the mouth	dh
ع	no close equivalent in English: a guttural sound in the back of the throat	'
غ	no close equivalent in English, but may be closely approximated by pronouncing it like the French /r/ in 'rouge'	gh
ف	/f/ as in *fill*, *effort* and *muff*	f

Arabic script	Pronunciation	Transliterated as:
ق	no close equivalent in English, but may be approximated by pronouncing /k/ farther back in the mouth	q
ك	/k/ as in *king, buckle* and *tack*	k
ل	/l/ as in *lap, halo*; in the word *Allah*, it becomes velarized as in *ball*	l
م	/m/ as in *men, simple* and *ram*	m
ن	/n/ as in *net, ant* and *can*	n
ـﺔ – ﻩ – ﻫ	/h/ as in *hat*; unlike /h/ in English, in Arabic /h/ is pronounced in medial and word-final positions as well	h
و	as in *wet* and *away*	w
و (as a vowel)	long u, as in *boot* and *too*	oo
ي	as in *yet* and *yard*	y
ي (as a vowel)	long e, as in *eat, beef* and *see*	ee
ء	glottal stop: may be closely approximated by pronouncing it like 't' in the Cockney English pronunciation of *butter*: *bu'er*, or the stop sound in *uh - oh!*	' (Omitted in initial position)

Diphthongs:

Arabic script	Pronunciation	Transliterated as:
و ، أَوَ	Long o, as in *owe, boat* and *go*	au, aw, ow
يَ ، أي	Long 'a', as in *able*, *rain* and *say*	ay, ai, ei

Diacritical marks (*tashkeel*):

Name of mark	Pronunciation	Transliterated as:
´ fathah	very short 'a' or schwa (unstressed vowel)	a
´ kasrah	shorter version of ee or schwa (unstressed vowel)	i
´ Dammah	shorter version of oo	u
´ shaddah	a doubled consonant is stressed in the word, and the length of the sound is also doubled	Double letter
° sukoon	no vowel sound between consonants or at the end of a word	Absence of vowel

About the word *Lord*

*T*he word *lord* in English has several related meanings. The original meaning is 'master' or 'ruler', and in this sense it is often used to refer to human beings: 'the lord of the mansion' or 'Lord So-and-so' (in the United Kingdom, for example). The word *Lord* with a capital L is used in the lexicon of Islam to refer to the One and Only God — Allah. In Islam, there is no ambiguity about the meaning of this word. While it is true that one may occasionally use the word *lord* (whether capitalized or not) to refer to a human being, in Islamic discourse the reference of this term is always clear from the context. Whereas for Christians, Hindus and other polytheists, the word *Lord* with a capital L may refer to Allah, to Jesus or to some imagined deity, for Muslims, there can be no plurality of meaning. Allah alone is the Lord, and the Lord is Allah — not Jesus, not Rama, not any other being.

THE EDITOR

Arabic honorific terms used in this book

(﷾): *Subḥânahu wa Ta'âlâ* — 'The Exalted'

(ﷺ): *Ṣalla-Allâhu 'alayhi wa sallam* — 'blessings and peace be upon him'

(﷫): *'alayhis-salâm* — 'Peace be upon him'

(﵁): *raḍiya Allâhu 'anhu* — 'may Allah be pleased with <u>him</u>'

(﵂): *raḍiya Allâhu 'anhâ* — 'may Allah be pleased with <u>her</u>'

Publisher's Note to the Third Edition

All praise and thanks belong to Allah alone, the One, the Almighty, and All-Merciful. Blessings and peace be upon Prophet Muhammad, the last of His Messengers and Prophets, his family, his Companions and all those who follow in his footsteps until the end of time.

Since *Bent Rib: A Journey through Women's Issues in Islam* was first written ten years ago, there have been new developments in many of the issues addressed by Huda Khattab. She has therefore revisited some of the issues and added new and important information to her treatment of each topic. She discusses changes in the ongoing discourse due to changing attitudes, the advent and spread of the Internet as a means for information exchange, and the increasing ability and willingness of Muslim women to network and to seek knowledge about matters that affect them.

It is our hope that this revised and expanded third edition of *Bent Rib* will be of greater benefit than the first — to many Muslim women and men.

May Allah bless the efforts of all who contributed to the production of this book, and may it be acceptable to Him.

Muhammad ibn 'Abdul-Muhsin Al-Tuwaijri

Managing Director,
International Islamic Publishing House
Riyadh, Saudi Arabia

بِسْــــمِ اللَّهِ الرَّحْمَنِ الرَّحِيمِ

In the Name of Allah, the All-Compassionate, All-Merciful

Dedication

To all my sisters in Islam who have been oppressed and who have suffered in the name of the religion that came to liberate them.

This is not the way it was meant to be.

May Allah guide us and unite us in true Islamic sisterhood and brotherhood, and may He grant a better tomorrow to our daughters — and our sons.

Huda Khattab

Acknowledgements

This book could not have been completed without the help of the following people, whose assistance is gratefully acknowledged:

Dr. S. M. Darsh and Dr. Suhaib Hasan, both of London, England, for patiently answering my many questions.

Sr. Aisha Rana of Toronto, Canada, for encouragement and the loan of several books and magazines.

Sr. Kathy Bullock of Toronto, Canada, for reviewing the manuscript and offering constructive criticism.

Last but by no means least: my husband (Nasiruddin al-Khattab), who offered advice, suggestions and help with Arabic sources, as well as distracting the children so that I could concentrate.

May Allah reward you all for your help: *Jazâkum Allâhu khayran.*

AUTHOR

Introduction

*T*his book is the outcome of several years' informal debate. Muslim women are continually discussing amongst themselves the issues addressed in this book, but the final impetus to put pen to paper came from a lengthy phone conversation that covered a number of these issues. I put the phone down and immediately scribbled down a list of issues. I had just spoken with a close friend who told me of yet another instance of wife-battering in the Muslim community, this time in a family in another town; a family with whom I was not well-acquainted, but who I knew were held in high esteem; people who, typically, one would never imagine as a household wherein violence was commonplace.

From domestic violence, we had moved on to discuss other feminine woes, and it struck me that there are several issues that are 'favourites' of our opponents, who use them against us at every opportunity. Even worse, the behaviour of Muslims may all too often only serve to reinforce the stereotypes. With the intention of putting our own house in order, it is time we examined exactly what Islam says about these matters. Then we can correct ourselves, and also have the confidence that we are equipped with the information with which to dispel the stereotypes.

This is also, in part, a very personal book. As a woman of Western origin, a convert to Islam, I have had to wrestle with many of the 'women in Islam' issues; and to a certain extent I am still, after over two decades in Islam, struggling to come to terms with one or two of them. It is the practices of Muslims that cause the problems; when one gets down to the nitty-gritty, the teachings of Islam itself are full of wisdom and common sense. The *ḥijāb*[1] was one of the easier issues to deal with. For me it was a liberation from the tyranny of Western fashion, the pressure on Western girls and women to 'look good', be skinny, and so on. The practice of total purdah, on the other hand, came as a great shock, both because I had grown up with the freedom to attend school, go to the library and corner store, visit friends, go to church, and so on, and because of the stories I had read of the women at the time of the Prophet (ﷺ), which depicted women who went out, for example, to attend the mosque, or to take part in battles.

Female circumcision was something else that was totally alien, although I soon found out that it was a popular stick with which to beat Islam and Muslims, in the early 80s at least. In more recent years, fortunately, the anti-FGM (female genital mutilation) activists have become more aware that they cannot blame this one on Islam, since it is neither sanctioned nor encouraged in our religion, and mutilation is expressly forbidden in Islamic law.

Of course, these are not the only issues that face Muslim women. The issues focused on here are those that tend to attract sometimes unwelcome attention from outsiders, which in turn means that we should find out the facts for ourselves. Muslim women are also concerned with other issues, such as the representation of Muslim women in the Western media, racism and discrimination, how to be able to wear the hijab and pray at work, at home, at school, and so forth. These are often problems that we have to contend with on a daily basis. Perhaps there is another book or two still to be written!

So this book is a reflection of my own journey through the troubled waters of 'woman in Islam'. I am well aware that I have embarked upon an adventure of learning that will be a lifetime odyssey. This book may be considered to be an interim report; I would not be so presumptuous as to say that it is the final word. Any errors are my own; may Allah forgive me, and may this work be acceptable to Him.

Huda Khattab

CHAPTER ONE

Going by the Book:
Qur'anic Interpretations

$\mathcal{T}$here are a number of issues surrounding women that are mentioned in the Qur'an and that are the subject of much debate. It is not unusual to see people from the 'anti-fundamentalists camp' obtain a copy of an English translation of the Qur'an, read through it, and pounce upon certain references as ammunition to use against Islam and Muslims. With little, if any, knowledge of Arabic, of the historical and social context in which the Qur'an was revealed, or of Islam as a way of life, they think that they have found the loose thread that will unravel the whole religion!

One of these references is the famous verse about 'beating' (*Qur'an 4: 34*), which will be discussed in the chapter on domestic violence (see Chapter 5). Here, we will look briefly at a few of the other issues surrounding women that appear in the Qur'an.

Qawwâmoon

﴿ٱلرِّجَالُ قَوَّٰمُونَ عَلَى ٱلنِّسَآءِ بِمَا فَضَّلَ ٱللَّهُ بَعْضَهُمْ عَلَىٰ بَعْضٍ وَبِمَآ أَنفَقُوا۟ مِنْ أَمْوَٰلِهِمْ فَٱلصَّٰلِحَٰتُ قَٰنِتَٰتٌ حَٰفِظَٰتٌ لِّلْغَيْبِ بِمَا حَفِظَ ٱللَّهُ ... ﴾

(سورة النِّسَاء: ٣٤)

❨Men are the protectors and maintainers [*qawwâmoon*] of women, because Allah has given the one more [strength] than the other, and because they support them from their means. Therefore the righteous women are devoutly obedient, and guard in [the husband's] absence what Allah would have them guard...❩

(Qur'an 4: 34)

Another widely-available translation, that by Marmaduke Pickthall, translates the first part of this verse as:

❨Men are in charge of women, because Allah has made the one of them to excel the other, and because they spend of their property [for the support of women]...❩

This word, *qawwâmoon*, has been interpreted in various ways. Ibn Katheer, pointing out that (in some schools of thought) the functions of being a prophet, an Imam and a religious judge are reserved exclusively for men, suggests that this means that men are superior to women.[2] However, we must also bear in mind the fact that the Qur'an clearly tells us that no one is automatically superior to another human being, except in the quality of *taqwâ*[3] *(Qur'an 49: 13)*. Some scholars expand on the idea of role differentiation by suggesting that as women's unique role is motherhood, so men should provide for women in order to free them from the burden of having to earn a living, thereby facilitating her devotion of time, energy and intellect to the sound raising of healthy, intelligent and committed Muslim children.[4]

When we look at the historical context in which this verse was revealed, the new order brought by Islam appears revolutionary. Prior to Islam, females in Arabia were devalued: if they were not murdered in infancy, they could expect a life of humiliation, being used and abused by men as 'playthings', and/or trapped in miserable marriages. Morals were lax, to say the least.

Islam made it quite clear that men had the responsibility to protect women (wives, daughters, and so on) from the predatory approaches of outsiders, whilst also maintaining them, that is, providing them with food, shelter, clothing, education, and so on. The woman, in turn, whilst enjoying security, had the responsibility of guarding her own chastity and morals. In this new, safer, climate, it was easier for her to do so; this also facilitated the preservation of lineage, which is so important in the Islamic scheme of things. (In Islam, the child has the right to know who his/her father is and to bear his name. This is one reason for the prohibition on sexual promiscuity and for the institution of marriage; within that institution, polygyny is permitted whereas polyandry is not, so that the paternity of a child will be known).

A further point to be remembered is that prior to the advent of Islam, the majority of cultures and religions held the belief that human perfection was possible only for men.[5] Women were very much sidelined and denied any significant role or opportunity for advancement in the intellectual and spiritual spheres. The early church, for example, spent a considerable amount of time making up its mind as to whether women actually possessed a soul. The Qur'an, on the other hand, made it abundantly clear that men and women are of equal worth, and that both are equally capable of spiritual success and of being rewarded accordingly:

﴿إِنَّ ٱلْمُسْلِمِينَ وَٱلْمُسْلِمَٰتِ وَٱلْمُؤْمِنِينَ وَٱلْمُؤْمِنَٰتِ وَٱلْقَٰنِتِينَ وَٱلْقَٰنِتَٰتِ وَٱلصَّٰدِقِينَ وَٱلصَّٰدِقَٰتِ وَٱلصَّٰبِرِينَ وَٱلصَّٰبِرَٰتِ وَٱلْخَٰشِعِينَ وَٱلْخَٰشِعَٰتِ وَٱلْمُتَصَدِّقِينَ وَٱلْمُتَصَدِّقَٰتِ وَٱلصَّٰٓئِمِينَ وَٱلصَّٰٓئِمَٰتِ وَٱلْحَٰفِظِينَ فُرُوجَهُمْ وَٱلْحَٰفِظَٰتِ وَٱلذَّٰكِرِينَ ٱللَّهَ كَثِيرًا وَٱلذَّٰكِرَٰتِ أَعَدَّ ٱللَّهُ لَهُم مَّغْفِرَةً وَأَجْرًا عَظِيمًا ﴿٣٥﴾﴾

(سورة الأحزاب: ٣٥)

《For Muslim men and women, for believing men and women, for devout men and women, for true men and women, for men and women who are patient and constant, for men and women who humble themselves, for men and women who give in charity, for men and women who fast [and deny themselves], for men and women who guard their chastity, and for men and women who engage much in Allah's praise, for them has Allah prepared forgiveness and great reward.》   *(Qur'an 33: 35)*

Marmaduke Pickthall translates qawwâmoon as 'in charge of', which perhaps is a reflection of the Islamic view that the husband is the head of the household. Islam prescribes that there should be one leader in every human organisation, be it a family, a group of travellers, an army or a nation; two or more 'bosses' would lead to an inability to resolve issues, which would in turn lead to chaos. Men are traditionally viewed as being generally more suited to leadership, which is why the position of imam, caliph, and head of state, for example, are viewed as being open only to males; but identifying the husband as the head of the household does not entitle the husband to be a little Hitler. Consultation and mutual decision-making are required, and the wife should have a say in any major decisions. Again, role differentiation is the name of the game. The husband-manager tends to be in charge of outside activities, whilst the wife tends to be in charge of internal household affairs; but it is far from cut-and-dried: each family will organise its affairs according to its own unique circumstances.

Obedience

Many throw up their hands in horror at the notion of obedience. In the West, it is regarded as hopelessly old-fashioned, or even demeaning. Western marriage vows have dropped the pledge to obey and promise only to 'love and honour'. Most Muslim scholars say that the wife should obey the husband, but this is on the condition that the husband's wishes do not go against Islam, because obedience to Allah (ﷻ) always takes priority. So if a husband tells his wife not to fast in Ramadan, not to pray, or not wear the hijab, then she can disobey him.

The prescription of obedience does not mean that marriage is supposed to be a master-slave relationship. As Mawdudi points out, the husband is not to use his 'superior position' (that is, his position of *qawwâmah*) as an excuse or means for oppressing his wife.[6] Contrary to widespread impressions of Islamic marriage (not to mention the practices of some Muslims), the Qur'anic view of marriage emphasises love, peace and harmony:

﴿وَمِنْ ءَايَتِهِۦٓ أَنْ خَلَقَ لَكُم مِّنْ أَنفُسِكُمْ أَزْوَٰجًا لِّتَسْكُنُوٓا إِلَيْهَا وَجَعَلَ بَيْنَكُم مَّوَدَّةً وَرَحْمَةً إِنَّ فِى ذَٰلِكَ لَأَيَٰتٍ لِّقَوْمٍ يَتَفَكَّرُونَ ٢١﴾

(سورة الرُّوم: ٢١)

﴿And among His Signs is this, that He created for you mates from among yourselves, that you may dwell in tranquillity with them, and He has put love and mercy between your [hearts]; verily in that are Signs for those who reflect.﴾   *(Qur'an 30: 21)*

Elsewhere, the relationship between husband and wife is described as one in which they are garments of one another *(Qur'an 2: 187)*. The Qur'anic descriptions of marriage, as it should be, paint a beautiful picture of harmony, comfort, companionship and support for both partners. This is not a prescription for dictatorship.

Another point to be made about Islamic teachings on obedience is that those who are in a position of obeying (whether in marriage or elsewhere) are not expected to be reduced to automata; they must still be aware of what they may be asked to do and decide for themselves whether it is right or not. Within the framework of marriage, a husband may ask his wife to do something that is forbidden; — for example, if they have a business, he may ask her to do something that is tantamount to cheating. In such a case, the woman is still responsible for her own decision. Cheating is forbidden, it goes against the commands of Allah, and she will have to answer for it in the hereafter, if not in this world. There is no room in Islam for 'only obeying orders'![7]

Darajah

Another reference that may be taken to mean that Islam prefers men to women occurs in Soorat al-Baqarah *(Qur'an 2: 228)*. Indeed many Muslims and even some Muslim scholars do interpret it in this way.[8] Taken in isolation, the phrase ❬*wa lir-rijâli 'alayhinna darajah*❭ might be taken as meaning just that. Yusuf Ali translates it as "men have a degree (of advantage) over them", whilst Pickthall's version is, "and men are a degree over them". Pickthall's translation is one that is somewhat troublesome, but it is worth pointing out that the Arabic *li* actually suggests 'having' rather than 'being' a degree above.

However, looking at phrases in isolation almost always leads to misunderstandings and hastily drawn, misbegotten, conclusions. The verse in question is no exception. What is often ignored by those who think this is about the relative worth of males versus females is the fact that this verse is not speaking in general terms: it is quite specific to the topic of divorce. The verse in full reads as follows:

﴿وَٱلْمُطَلَّقَٰتُ يَتَرَبَّصْنَ بِأَنفُسِهِنَّ ثَلَٰثَةَ قُرُوٓءٍ وَلَا يَحِلُّ لَهُنَّ أَن يَكْتُمْنَ مَا خَلَقَ ٱللَّهُ

فِى أَرْحَامِهِنَّ إِن كُنَّ يُؤْمِنَّ بِٱللَّهِ وَٱلْيَوْمِ ٱلْآخِرِ وَبُعُولَتُهُنَّ أَحَقُّ بِرَدِّهِنَّ فِى ذَلِكَ إِنْ
أَرَادُوٓا۟ إِصْلَٰحًا وَلَهُنَّ مِثْلُ ٱلَّذِى عَلَيْهِنَّ بِٱلْمَعْرُوفِ وَلِلرِّجَالِ عَلَيْهِنَّ دَرَجَةٌ وَٱللَّهُ عَزِيزٌ
حَكِيمٌ ۞

(سورة البَقَرَة: ٢٢٨)

《Divorced women shall wait concerning themselves for three monthly periods. Nor is it lawful for them to hide what Allah has created in their wombs, if they have faith in Allah and the Last Day. And their husbands have the better right to take them back in that period, if they wish for reconciliation. And women shall have rights similar to the rights against them, according to what is equitable, but men have a degree [of advantage] over them. And Allah is Exalted in Power, Wise.》 *(Qur'an 2: 228)*

This "degree of advantage" is explained in various ways. Aminah Wadud-Muhsin limits it to the topic under discussion in the verse itself, namely divorce: men are able to pronounce divorce (*talâq*) by themselves, whereas women who seek divorce (in Arabic this sort of divorce is known as *khul'*) need some outside assistance or intervention (that is, a judge).[9] Yusuf Ali suggests that it is due to economic differences; men are usually the breadwinners, so a woman without her own independent income may well be at a disadvantage.[10] Another suggestion is that the divorced male has the advantage of being able to remarry immediately, whilst the woman must wait at least three months: the *'iddah*, or waiting period.[11] However, the differences are to be regarded as functional and practical (the division of labour, again). This verse is not general in application; it refers only to divorce. "*Darajah*" cannot be taken to mean that men are intrinsically better than women. The only factor that makes any person, regardless of gender, class or race, better than another, is *taqwâ* (*Qur'an 49: 13*).

However the advantage is interpreted, it still comes with responsibility: men are told to treat women kindly and decently even if the marriage is breaking down, and even if they dislike their wives:

﴿... وَعَاشِرُوهُنَّ بِالْمَعْرُوفِ فَإِن كَرِهْتُمُوهُنَّ فَعَسَىٰ أَن تَكْرَهُوا شَيْئًا وَيَجْعَلَ
اللَّهُ فِيهِ خَيْرًا كَثِيرًا ١٩﴾

(سورة النِّساء: ١٩)

﴿... Live with them on a footing of kindness and equity. If you take a dislike to them it may be that you dislike a thing, and Allah brings about through it a great deal of good.﴾   *(Qur'an 4: 19)*

Whatever the case, men have no right to mistreat women. Even the well-known permission to 'strike' the wife in the case of her extreme misconduct may be interpreted as a symbolic gesture: scholars place restrictions on this version of corporal punishment and remind Muslims that the Prophet (ﷺ) never raised his hand against a woman.

Has Allah given more to men than to women?

﴿انظُرْ كَيْفَ فَضَّلْنَا بَعْضَهُمْ عَلَىٰ بَعْضٍ وَلَلْآخِرَةُ أَكْبَرُ دَرَجَاتٍ وَأَكْبَرُ تَفْضِيلًا
٢١﴾

(سورة الإسرَاء: ٢١)

﴿See how We have bestowed more on some than on others; but verily the Hereafter is more in rank and gradation and more in excellence.﴾   *(Qur'an 17: 21)*

This is another verse that may be taken as 'proof' of the inherent superiority of men over women. However, the verse is saying no such thing! Far from discussing family matters, marital rules or gender roles, this verse appears in a passage of Soorat al-

Isrâ' *(Qur'an 17: 18-22)* that discusses the greater scheme of things, why the wicked are often seen to prosper in this world, and how justice will finally be done in the hereafter, for which believers should always strive.

The bounties of Allah are bestowed on all, Muslims and non-Muslims, good and bad alike. Some are given more than others, in all aspects of life and, as Yusuf Ali points out,[12] it is the spiritual gifts such as faith and guidance that will ultimately be the most valuable. The idea that Allah has bestowed on some more than on others means that in any given instance, a man may excel over other men, and over women; similarly, in some aspects a woman may excel over other women, and over men. It is an easily-observed fact of life that if a person excels in one thing he or she may well be lacking in another; for example, a rich man may suffer ill-health. It cannot be taken to mean that all men are better than all women just because they are men!

Women: concerned only with frivolities?

❨What! Has He taken daughters out of what He Himself has created, and granted to you sons for choice? When news is brought to one of them of [the birth of] what he sets up as a likeness to [Allah] Most Gracious, his face darkens, and he is filled with inward grief! Is then one brought up among trinkets, and unable to give a clear account in a dispute [to be associated with Allah]?❩ *(Qur'an 43: 16-18)*

If this passage were a commandment, telling Muslims to raise their daughters to be concerned with nothing more than trivia, then perhaps it could be taken as indicative of male superiority and female inferiority. However, this is not the case. This chapter exposes the falsehood of other systems of worship:

the verse preceding this passage condemns the 'deification' of prophets. Verses 16-18 specifically address the pre-Islamic Arabs, who believed in a number of deities, including goddesses who they regarded as 'daughters of Allah'. In real life, they despised females, abusing them and casting them aside, going into mourning at the birth of a daughter, killing female infants, and so on. Given that this was the case, it was particularly blasphemous, to use Yusuf Ali's words,[13] that they would ascribe daughters to Allah when they desired only sons: how dare they attribute to Allah that which they themselves held in contempt!

So the phrase "brought up among trinkets..." is a reflection of the historical and cultural context in which the verse was revealed. It may be regarded as rhetorical rather than telling us that this is how women should be.[14] Early Muslim history shows us quite clearly that women who are held up to us as examples to be emulated — Khadeejah, 'Â'ishah, Fâṭimah (may Allah be pleased with them) — were concerned with much more than trivia: their interests were to learn more about Islam, to perform the Ḥajj and the *'umrah*,[15] to fight in jihad, and so on.

Menstruation

Another issue that causes misunderstanding, even among Muslims, is menstruation. The common assumption is that Islam regards menstruating women as unclean, so she must not touch the Qur'an or a prayer mat, or enter a mosque, and so on. I remember meeting some Muslim women who thought that it is inappropriate to apply henna when menstruating because, as henna takes a week or two to wear off, it would somehow be 'impure' and there would therefore be some impurity left even after performing *ghusl*![16] For the same reason, they would change and wash whatever clothes they were wearing as soon as the period ended, even if the clothes were otherwise clean. These are surely ideas that have crept into Islam from other sources, such as Hindu and Jewish traditions.

The Qur'an does refer to menstruation, in the following verse:

وَيَسْـَٔلُونَكَ عَنِ ٱلْمَحِيضِ قُلْ هُوَ أَذًى فَٱعْتَزِلُوا ٱلنِّسَآءَ فِى ٱلْمَحِـيضِ وَلَا تَقْرَبُوهُنَّ حَتَّىٰ يَطْهُرْنَ فَإِذَا تَطَهَّرْنَ فَأْتُوهُنَّ مِنْ حَيْثُ أَمَرَكُمُ ٱللَّهُ إِنَّ ٱللَّهَ يُحِبُّ ٱلتَّوَّٰبِينَ وَيُحِبُّ ٱلْمُتَطَهِّرِينَ ۝ (سورة البَقَرَة: ٢٢٢)

❴They ask you concerning women's courses. Say: They are a hurt and a pollution [*adhâ*]: so keep away from women in their courses and do not approach them until they are clean. But when they have purified themselves, you may approach them in any manner, time or place ordained for you by Allah. For Allah loves those who turn to Him constantly and He loves those who keep themselves pure and clean.❵ *(Qur'an 2: 222)*

Other translators vary in the rendering of *adhâ*, interpreting it as 'illness' (Pickthall) or 'a state of impurity' (Mawdudi). This causes much debate because the assumption that the entire woman is rendered impure by menstruation may be taken to infer that women are therefore inferior or less worthy because of this recurring state of impurity that may make them unable to pray for one week out of every four.

However, singling out menstruation in this way is quite unfair. The idea of 'purity' refers to the state of 'ritual' cleanliness needed for Muslims to perform acts of worship, for example, formal prayer (*salât*) and touching the Qur'an. Both men and women are subject to bodily functions that necessitate *wuḍoo'*[17] or ghusl. In this regard, an Arabic-speaking Muslim (whether male or female) may, if called to come to pray when he/she is unable to because of not having wuḍoo' or ghusl, may tell his/her companions, "I am not pure." This is meant to indicate his/her temporary condition, and does not mean that the entire person is impure, unclean or unworthy!

The authors of *Tafseer al-Jalâlayn* point out that it is the part of the body in which menstruation is taking place that is impure,[18] which does not make the whole person impure or unworthy. 'Â'ishah (⁕) narrated a hadith describing how the Prophet (⁕) asked her to pass his prayer mat to him. When she pointed out that she was menstruating, he said, «Your menstruation is not in your hands!»[19]

Indeed, the Prophet (⁕) and the Companions (may Allah be pleased with them all) adopted a very down-to-earth attitude towards the whole issue of menstruation. Far from regarding a menstruating women as a virtual untouchable, Islam regards her as a normal human being who is currently suffering a particular kind of discomfort. Thus 'Â'ishah (⁕) described how the Prophet (⁕) lay with his head in her lap and recited verses of the Qur'an whilst she was menstruating,[20] and on the occasion referred to above asked her to pass his prayer mat to him. Although she was menstruating, her hand was not regarded as being too unclean to pass the object required, even a prayer mat.

In fact, the rulings surrounding the menstruating woman are very straightforward and simple, unlike other faith systems where she may be banished to a separate bedroom, forced to sit and eat alone, forbidden to prepare food for others, and so on. During her period, a woman is not allowed to pray the formal prayers — ṣalâh, to fast or to touch the muṣ-ḥaf, or to have intercourse with her husband. However, according to some schools of thought, she may enter the mosque (so long as her flow is not so heavy as to risk leaking onto the floor and thus dirtying it), attend study circles and gatherings, and even to read and recite the Qur'an for the purpose of studying or teaching.[21] She is encouraged to attend the *'Eid*[22] prayers (without joining in the prayer) and join in the *takbeerât*[23]; so she may still attend gatherings, enjoy fellowship with others, learn, study, and so on. Within the marital framework, she may still enjoy physical closeness with her husband; all that is forbidden is actual intercourse.

Narrated 'Abdullâh ibn Sa'd al-Anṣâri: «'Abdullâh asked the Messenger of Allah (ﷺ): What is lawful for me to do with my wife when she is menstruating? He replied: What is above the waist-wrapper is lawful for you. The narrator also mentioned (the lawfulness of) eating with a woman in menstruation, and he transmitted the tradition in full.»[24]

These rulings in fact indicate a special kind of compassion shown towards Muslim women. Menstruation is often a burden and a nuisance with heavy bleeding, cramps, and pain, and this is recognised by Islam. So it can be seen as something of a mercy that the woman is relieved of some of her duties at this time. Indeed, many Muslim women refer to their periods, colloquially, as 'being on holiday'. As far as sex is concerned, it would surely be unpleasant and unhealthy to have intercourse at this time, so this may be regarded as a mercy to both men and women in that it saves them from exposure to potential harm.

Summary

Islam is not the rigid, harsh, misogynist faith portrayed by the media. The Qur'anic ideal is one of egalitarianism where each individual will ultimately be judged on his or her own merits.

Whilst Islam seeks to set limits for human behaviour, offering regulations and guidelines, the intent is not to oppress one group or favour one over another. In instances where men may be seen to have an advantage, a closer examination of the facts will show that this is not a licence to oppress women, and that the privilege is accompanied by greater responsibilities. Islam recognises the human experience and provides a practical, humane and attainable prescription for life. The Qur'an explicitly addresses women and declares them to be spiritually equal to men. Viewed against the historical background of the seventh century CE, what the Qur'an brought to women was nothing short of revolutionary. Nevertheless, it must be acknowledged that the reality has not matched its ideal. As I will discuss in the coming chapters, Muslims often fall short in their practice of what Islam tells them to do, especially with regard to the treatment of women.

CHAPTER TWO

Partners for Life or
Three Strikes and You're Out?
Marriage and Divorce

$\mathcal{T}$he tabloid image of Islam presents many negative stereotypes of marriage: under-aged girls wed to men old enough to be their grandfathers; fourteen and fifteen-year-old girls taken on 'holidays' to the parents' homeland, where they are then forced into marriage to a cousin or other relative they have never seen before; young girls imported to the West from rural villages, unable to speak a word of English, never venturing beyond the cocoon of the family or community, terrified and alone when, for example, a medical emergency thrusts them into the outside world; traditional-minded men brought over as husbands for girls who, after growing up and being educated in the West, and perhaps expecting to have a job or career, may suddenly be expected to stay at home and be meek and submissive.

Then there are the husbands who are shirking their responsibilities and failing to provide adequate support to their wives and children. Many of those women end up turning to government hand-outs to keep body and soul together. It is not unknown for a husband even to go as far as demanding "rent" from his wife to live in his house.

When a marriage goes wrong, so the popular notion goes, the man at least has an easy way out. He can declare " *Ṭâliq* ! *Ṭâliq* !! *Ṭâliq* !!!" — a traditional and widespread version of divorce that is in fact un-Islamic. 'Ṭâliq' literally means 'You are divorced', and is the utterance whereby a man may actually divorce his wife, whereas the word 'talâq' means 'divorce' (the noun) denoting the legal process. If a man divorces his wife, she must return to her family, who may not want her back because the stigma is so great: how will they marry off any other daughters if this one is a 'failure'? If a man can divorce the wife at whim like this, she must forever be walking on eggshells so as not to arouse his wrath and risk being cast aside, becoming an object of scorn and pity. Many women trapped in miserable marriages may want to escape, but they do not want to live alone: they are well aware of Islamic teachings that place such an emphasis on marriage. They wish that they could be free to find a happier match elsewhere. Women have their own needs for love and companionship, security and protection, for material and moral support, and for a father-figure for their children. They want to find all this through permissible means. However, if you ask them why they do not ask for a divorce and get out, they sigh and tell you, "Who else would have me, with this number of kids? Better the 'devil' you know...!"

Such goings-on are not unique to any particular community, and certainly not just to Muslims. One should probably be resigned to the fact that they are part of the human condition! This does not mean that such instances of abuse should be excused. The distressing fact is that in too many cases, religion is used to justify and condone, or at least excuse, what all too often amounts to nothing less than the oppression of women. Detractors then come along and find plenty of ammunition for their cause; they can claim that Islam is a cruel religion that oppresses women, and they will find no lack of 'evidence' to support their claims.

It all boils down to the yawning chasm that exists between the teachings and ideals of Islam and the practices of many Muslims. Customs and cultural practices have arisen (or been allowed to continue as a carryover from the previous religion/ culture of lands to which Islam spread) that are contrary to the actual teachings of Islam. Throughout the world, the dominant Western culture is also having a major impact on the way things are done. Marriage and family life, which are so central to the stability of a community, are given such importance in the Islamic scheme of things that marriage is described as being "half the faith"[1]. This is the fact that should be recognised by all Muslims, whether they come from Western or from other cultures.

Choosing a partner

Let us start at the beginning: the selection of a marriage partner. The Islamic way is diametrically opposed to the Western way. Western families, to a large extent, leave their children to sink or swim in the nerve-wracking and confusing world of dates and boyfriend/girlfriend. Western books and magazines are full of tales of woe and letters to 'agony aunts' and advice columnists describing the heartache caused when boy-meets-girl and one of them is looking for a lifetime commitment whilst the other just wants a 'good time'. It's a guessing game that resembles a kind of romantic Russian roulette, and although there may occasionally be a father who demands to know whether the young man's intentions towards his daughter are 'honourable', too many young people must negotiate the minefield alone. Too many marriages end up where, once the euphoria of falling in love has worn off, the partners find that they have very little in common, and hardly enough to base a lifetime commitment on.

In contrast, the Islamic way is to arrange a match between compatible partners. Muslims are not allowed to date or engage in pre-marital intimacy (not even holding hands or kissing). Parents, relatives, elders and/or close and trusted friends will scout for prospective partners, check out their background and negotiate arrangements. Ideally, young people have the security of knowing that their parents or guardians have their best interests at heart and will find the right person for them. The burden is lifted from their shoulders, to some extent, and they know that they need not take numerous chances and risks in hopes of finding Mr. or Ms. Right.

No forced marriages in Islam

Arranged, however, does not mean forced. The prospective partners, especially the girl, have the right to say 'no', and this is to be respected by the parents or guardians. It is her right to refuse. There are sound hadiths that show that the Prophet (ﷺ) annulled marriages in cases where a girl or woman had been forced to marry a partner she disliked.[2] A few years ago, the story of a Scottish woman of Pakistani descent who had been forced into a marriage to a man from 'back home' against her will, and had been under-age (according to Western law) at the time, hit the headlines when her marriage was annulled in the Scottish courts. She was stigmatised and ostracised by her community, but her case brought the issue of forced marriages into the public eye.

But what about romance?

Many Westerners find this way of arranging marriages to be totally unromantic, and even rather odd; but if you take the time to explain it, they may begin to see the wisdom behind it. Muslims who are unduly influenced by movies and novels may also feel some kind of longing for 'romance'; they forget that these works of fiction exaggerate, and are not representative of real life. The Islamic way certainly involves much businesslike talk and negotiation of conditions, and the prospective partners may 'interview' one another, which makes it all seem more like a boardroom deal than the romance of the century. People who have over-indulged in Hollywood love stories and Mills & Boon or Harlequin romances may well find it all quite weird, but surely it is better to 'lay all one's cards on the table' (to borrow a phrase!) from the outset than to find things out the hard way and have unpleasant surprises later on. That is not to say that nasty surprises never happen in arranged marriages either: everyone concerned must be willing to ask — and answer — comprehensive questions about background, aspirations, hopes, plans, and so forth.[3]

This businesslike approach does not entirely rule out 'romance' altogether, however. If a young person particularly likes someone whom he/she may know through the circle of relatives and family friends, youth activities at the mosque, or even from school or university, then there is no harm in asking parents to pursue the matter via appropriate channels — provided, of course, that no improper behaviour results. Such cases do happen, but, sadly, problems may arise when the person liked by the youngster is of a different ethnic background: many Muslim families cannot imagine marrying their children to someone of a different background. This is, of course, a totally un-Islamic attitude that verges on racism. Many matches between people of the same background occur because of the natural patterns of contact between people, but we should not isolate ourselves from other Muslims, and we should not close minds to the possibility of a mixed match.

On the lines of 'romance', there is an interesting trend among some Muslim families. A couple of generations ago, marriages would be arranged and solemnised without the couple never even seeing one another until after the marriage contract had been signed, when they would be expected to cohabit and set up home together immediately — quite an ordeal for both partners! (It is also un-Islamic, as Islam clearly gives the prospective partners the right to meet and see each other so that they may decide whether they are at all attracted to the prospective partner). Nowadays, some families are choosing to contract the marriage, but then allow the couple some space, each partner remaining in the family home for a few months more until, with a huge party for family and friends, the establishment of a new household is announced and celebrated. This arrangement, which is akin to an engagement, gives the couple some space to meet without the girl having to always wear her hijab in front of him, and allows the couple to get to know each other a little better, as the marriage contract is already done and they are at liberty to do so. If the partners are in different countries, perhaps waiting to process immigration papers, this is a time when they can write letters to one another or phone one another (parents can expect a sharp rise in phone bills!). Then when the time comes for them to set up house together, they will not be complete strangers to one another.

Early marriage

Another alternative to common attitude and practice, of interest to many Muslim parents in the west — where temptations and pressures are, perhaps, greatest — is early marriage. This may be regarded as pretty 'radical', as the widely-held notion is that it is better to wait until young people, especially men, have completed their education and established themselves, put down a deposit on a house, bought a car, and so on. While the intention may be good — namely to have some kind of stability and security before marrying and starting a family — this approach puts almost unbearable pressure on young people, who are still faced with constant temptation to stray, combined with their own powerful youthful urges, but who are being told to wait until they are 'established' before they can have a legitimate outlet for those very human feelings. If a person has chosen a career that needs lengthy study before they can work, he (or indeed she) may well be nearly 30 before they can think of marrying, which, assuming that puberty begins around age 15, amounts to half a lifetime spent having to resist a great deal of temptation. Should we be surprised if many stumble off the 'straight path' under such conditions?

Recognising the pressures that their children are under, some Muslim parents are now seriously considering the idea of allowing their children to marry young, and encouraging the young couple to study and grow together. They will thus have a permissible outlet for all those urges (which will have a beneficial, calming effect!) and also a partner to study with or to offer moral and practical support whilst they set up a business or establish themselves in their chosen career. Some families are even ensuring that the marriage contract includes a clause that guarantees that the wife will be able to complete her studies (some women even stipulate that this means right up to a PhD).

However, early marriage can give cause for concern when it is used to 'get girls out of danger'. This attitude may be found among some parents in ethnic communities where early marriage is a tradition, and also among immigrant parents who fear the un-Islamic influences that their daughters are exposed to in high school. Early marriage is thus a way to cut the schooling and remove the child from the perceived danger, in some cases by sending the daughter back to the homeland to marry. Such marriages are often forced, and deny the girl not only her say in the choice of a marriage partner, but also her right to an education — both of which are rights clearly given by Islam. No youngster should be forced into an early marriage, and parents must ensure that their children (sons as well as daughters) are given a sound Islamic education and a positive sense of their Muslim identity. Whether or not an early marriage is arranged, girls should be allowed and encouraged to pursue an education and develop their full potential.

Prevention is better than cure

While considering the choice of a marriage partner, we should remember that prevention is better than cure. In other words, the more care we exercise in choosing a compatible partner, the less likely the risk of the marriage hitting the rocks later on, *inshâ' Allâh* (God willing). Divorce is permitted in Islam, of course, but it is a disliked option to be used as a last resort. Any Muslim who is getting married should be doing so with the attitude and intention that this is a commitment for life.

Just because a person is from 'back home', that is no guarantee that he or she is the best partner for your daughter or son, even if he or she is a relative. Of course, many such matches are a great success, but it is the ones that fail that we usually hear about ('no news is good news'). Children who grow up in the West are very different from their cousins who grow up in the homeland. If parents have kept the language and culture alive in the home and have taken the children to visit the homeland or welcomed visitors from back home, then this will make such matches easier. I have met numerous girls of Pakistani descent in the UK who have willingly chosen to marry someone from back home; some will ask their parents to arrange such a match, and some choose to return to the homeland and live there rather in the West. In other cases however, the partners may be light years apart, despite the fact that they may be related. They may not even speak the same language, and their marriage may be an unhappy and isolating experience for both partners. Many couples in such circumstances manage to overcome these difficulties and come to care for one another deeply, but too many others will endure nothing but misery.

There is a lot to be said in favour of mixed marriages, especially when it comes to breaking down barriers and strengthening the ties between Muslims, but in arranging such a match, caution is appropriate. If a prospective partner is of the same ethnic or cultural background, it is relatively easy to carry out some kind of background check; in many Muslim countries the social networks facilitate such 'vetting' of prospective partners. In the melting pots (or mosaics, if you prefer) of Western cities, where the Muslim community may resemble a microcosm of the Islamic world (plus converts from the local communities), the variety of backgrounds makes this checking somewhat harder in the case of prospective mixed marriages.

Compatibility

Some Muslim scholars have recommended that there be some measure of social compatibility (for example, in status, class, wealth, education, and so forth) between marriage partners, advice which is an application of 'worldly wisdom' and a recognition of the tendency of human societies to organise themselves into strata.[4] The suggestion is that, in general, it is preferable for the husband to have the 'higher' status, in part because his role as head of the household may be undermined if the wife looks down on him because of his lack of education, wealth, and so on, and this can lead to instability in the marriage. During the lifetime of the Prophet (ﷺ), the unhappy marriage and eventual divorce between Zaynab bint Jaḥsh (a noblewoman) and Zayd ibn Ḥârithah (an ex-slave) is an example of the need for social class compatibility in a marriage. Nevertheless, the Islamic ideal of egalitarianism permits marriages that cross these barriers, and with a good amount of faith, patience, tolerance and love, 'unlikely' matches can succeed.

This compatibility is possible to achieve in a mixed match, and indeed may contribute to the success of such a marriage. Individuals who are interested in finding a partner from a different background should be encouraged to have a 'support team' that will protect their interests and do the necessary background checking. Many of those raised as Muslims will have their parents and families around, of course; but overseas students, refugees, and converts to Islam may well need to find someone, perhaps a close friend or trusted elder, to support them. Those who take part in arranging such matches should also be prepared to make a long-term commitment to offering ongoing support and help, should it be needed.

Compatibility goes beyond equivalency of socio-economic status, of course. Level of education (or educational aspirations) are also important, as are ideas about the number of children hoped for, and the city or country in which partners want to settle. Level of commitment to Islam is another very important consideration, but the school of thought (madh-hab) followed by the other person and types of Islamic activity and involvement should also be borne in mind. In fact, prospective partners should also give some thought to one another's views on apparently trivial matters such as their views on having pets, smoking, and so on.

Divorce

However careful we are in choosing marriage partners, mistakes do occur, and some marriages do not succeed. Instead of imprisoning two people in misery and, perhaps finding themselves pushed to commit unlawful deeds, Islam permits divorce as a way out so that each partner may be free to find a more compatible match elsewhere. Sadly, however, Muslim communities have attached a huge stigma to divorce, and especially to the divorced woman. No one wants to marry a divorced woman, especially if she has children. Divorced men, however, do not have quite such a hard time. The fear of this shame and stigma make many unhappy women afraid to flee their miserable marriages, so they stay put and suffer.

Many, many misunderstandings surround the issue of divorce in Islam. Many people believe, incorrectly, that a man need merely pronounce the words "I divorce you" three times to his wife for the marriage to be over. Such a system would leave women in a constant state of anxiety, lest they offend the husband and incite him to pronounce the fateful "*Ṭâliq* ! *Ṭâliq* !! *Ṭâliq* !!!" ('You are divorced!', repeated three times), that would leave her out in the cold. Such a system would, of course, be grossly unfair to women. But this is contrary to the *Sunnah*.[5]

We will look briefly at the Islamic teachings concerning divorce, but any reader who finds herself/himself in a situation where divorce seems to be the only option is **strongly advised to consult with a reputable Islamic scholar and/or Islamic social services provider or helpline before taking action.**

A certain amount of confusion is caused for English-speaking Muslims by the fact that the word 'divorce', which signifies the break-up of a marriage, is the word used to translate the Arabic term *ṭalâq*. This equating of the *ṭalâq* with divorce tends to mask the fact that there is another word in Arabic, *khul'*, which may also be translated as divorce. For the reminder of this discussion, we will use the Arabic words to make the distinction clear. The ensuing sections will clarify these terms and what they mean.

Ṭalâq

Ṭalâq (**the** divorce word, for many Muslims) refers to divorce initiated by the husband. This is the divorce that can be repeated up to a maximum of three times, but they are not meant to be simultaneous. The thrice uttered 'instant divorce' is in fact a form of innovation that was known, but certainly not approved, in early Islamic times. The Caliph 'Umar ibn al-Khaṭṭâb (رضي الله عنه) is known to have had men whipped for divorcing their wives in this fashion.

Ṭalâq works as follows: If a marriage is floundering, the husband may make a single pronouncement of divorce, as long as certain important conditions are met (see below). The 'iddah, or 'waiting period', then begins — a time-span that is defined as being three menstrual cycles. The purpose of this is to establish whether or not the wife is pregnant; if she is, then the 'iddah lasts until delivery. If the woman has passed menopause, her 'iddah is three months. During the 'iddah, she remains in the marital home, and the husband is obliged to pay her living expenses, providing food and other necessities. The hope, of course, is that a reconciliation may come about, possibly through the mediation of relatives. If, before the 'iddah is over, they have marital relations, then the marriage is resumed. If the 'iddah expires, but they wish to remain married, a new marriage contract is needed.

However, some men are cruel enough to repeat this process an indefinite number of times, thus keeping the unfortunate wife in a state of mental and emotional insecurity and instability, and unable to seek a happier life elsewhere. For this reason, Islam imposed a limit, which may be described in vernacular terms as "three strikes and you're out!"[6] If this ṭalâq happens for a third time, it is deemed irrevocable. The couple cannot remarry unless the wife marries another man, consummates that marriage, then is divorced or widowed. This might sound like a loop-hole at first, but the scholars are quite adamant that arranging such a marriage just to facilitate re-marriage to the first husband is a travesty that is to be condemned; the Prophet (ﷺ) cursed those who took the law so lightly in this fashion.[7] Each marriage is to be taken seriously, and is to be embarked upon with the intention of a lifetime commitment; divorce is a last resort if things go wrong. The message is that divorce is a serious matter, with serious consequences. Both partners should think, not of short-term gains and scoring points over one another, but of the long-term consequences; and for Muslims that means not only this world but also the next.

It is also important to be aware of the conditions for ṭalâq.[8] No pronouncement of ṭalâq can be made during a woman's menstrual period or post-natal bleeding. If ṭalâq is to be pronounced, it must be done after the women has cleansed herself (ghusl) following the end of her period, and before any intercourse takes place. This rules out any possibility of ṭalâq being uttered in the heat of the moment, at a time when the husband may feel frustrated and angry because of the restrictions imposed on sexual intimacy when the woman has her menses or post-natal bleeding.

Defining a specific time and specific conditions means that the husband who is contemplating ṭalâq is likely to have to wait a while; this 'breathing-space' will allow both partners the chance to calm down, think rationally about the situation and, possibly, to be reconciled.

Khul'

There are, however, men who will keep a wife in a miserable marriage. Such a man does not care for the poor woman, but his male pride cannot bear to let her go and find a better life elsewhere. Some of these men may well be on some kind of twisted 'power trip', as is borne out by beatings and abuse inflicted on their wives. The wife may ask for a divorce (ṭalâq), but he refuses. In such a case, the woman has the right to initiate the divorce herself. This is known as *khul'*. However, scholars point out that it is forbidden to mistreat a woman so as to force her to initiate khul', thereby making her pay the financial penalty.[9]

Khul' is also the means by which a woman may extricate herself from a marriage in which she is unhappy, even if the husband is not particularly at fault. Such was the case of Thâbit's wife, who found no fault in his personality, but could not bear how he looked and was unable to reconcile herself to his appearance.[10]

If she chooses to take this option, the woman may have to forfeit all or part of her dowry (which, in some of the worst cases, may be a small price to pay). There has been some controversy over this issue, with the impression being given that women may be 'taken for a ride' or cheated out of their money when they seek to initiate khul', because of the ruling that they must give up the dowry. Those who are guilty of abusing this rule should examine their consciences and think about how they will answer for it in the hereafter. In fact, the scholars apply a kind of sliding scale to the amount that the wife must forfeit. If she is acting on a whim with no reasonable grounds, then she may be penalised by having to repay the entire dowry, or sometimes more. If she is escaping from an abusive marriage, or can prove misconduct on the part of her husband, a just judge or authority would not penalise her in such a way; she may pay back only part of the dowry, or even none at all.[11]

There is a difference of opinion regarding the length of the waiting period in case of khul'. A minority of scholars suggest that it is only one menstrual cycle; the majority, however, say that the waiting period in this case is the same as that in the case of ṭalâq.[12] Khul' is also regarded as being irrevocable.[13]

Summary

Marriage and divorce are not matters to be taken lightly. Islam views them as being of great importance, as the family is the basic unit upon which the community, nation and *Ummah*[14] are built. So great care is to be exercised in selecting a partner with whom to build a new family. The Islamic ideal of marriage is one of harmony, love and tranquillity, not a battleground or a master-slave scenario. If things go awry, there are guidelines to bring about a reconciliation, but divorce is available as a last resort. Traditional practices have tended to distort the application of divorce, so Muslims need to acquaint themselves with the true teachings of Islam. There are various ways of dissolving a marriage, and it cannot be said often enough that those who find themselves in such a situation are strongly urged to consult with scholars and community elders who are knowledgeable and experienced in dealing with such issues.

CHAPTER THREE

Domestic Slaves and Baby Factories?
The Role of Muslim Women

" *How* could an intelligent woman like you choose a religion like Islam?!" Many convert sisters have been asked this question over the years, and it usually stems from the questioner's perceptions of the treatment of women in Islam. People, it seems, just cannot accept the fact that educated, Western women will embrace Islam of their own free will.

Part of the problem is the fact that many people (including Muslims) think that the Muslim woman's purpose in life is to be 'pregnant, barefoot and in the kitchen'. I have met Muslim women who spend hours and hours, every day, in the kitchen, preparing traditional food from scratch, because their husbands insist that they must have freshly-cooked food each day, that they will only eat their own 'ethnic' food, and so forth. These women may be living in an isolated nuclear family situation, far from relatives and with none of the extended family support (or even servants) that in the past would have meant that someone was available to tend the bubbling pots on the stove whilst the mother attended to her crying baby. Even so, the husband will assume a 'lord and master' role and demand his curry and *roti*, or *kibbeh*[1] and *melokhia*, not lifting a finger to help whilst his wife struggles to juggle.

Muslims living in the West are also confronted with the fact that the housewife/mother role tends to be looked down on there, and with the overwhelming influence of the media, it is hardly surprising that such attitudes are invading Muslim communities as well. Muslim girls growing up in the West are being educated in a system that is prepares girls as well as boys to expect to look for work and have a career; yet at home, many Muslim girls find that they are burdened with household chores whilst their brothers are free to concentrate on their homework, or even to just mess around. Not surprisingly, these girls feel resentment, which — as religion may well be cited to justify the situation — may be directed against Islam, thus alienating such girls from their own religion.

Unpaid domestic servants?

But does Islam really say that women should live a life of drudgery? What do scholars have to say about women and household tasks? The scholars vary in their viewpoints from those who say that women must serve their husbands, to those who say that there is no such obligation and that the husband should meet his wife's every need so that she will not be obliged to work.[2] There is even a suggestion that the food provided by the husband should be already cooked! This is the view of Ibn Ḥazm, who suggests that the woman's duties are only: to treat her husband kindly; not to fast voluntarily in his presence without his permission; not to allow any strangers (especially non-*mahram*[3] males, but also any females that he disapproves of) to enter the home if they are not welcomed by the husband; not to deny herself to him any time he wishes; and to protect the wealth he has entrusted to her. There is no mention here of cooking, serving his guests, washing his clothes, or other such duties.[4]

However, scholars recognise that cultural and social patterns influence the way husbands and wives live together, and they acknowledge that in the majority of cases, from time immemorial, men's role has been outside the home whilst women's work has been focused on the home.[5]

Women's work in Madinah

When we look at the first Muslim community, in Madinah, we find that the women did in fact do a great deal of the domestic work. Asmâ' (⬥), the wife of Zubayr ibn 'Awwâm and sister of 'Â'ishah (⬥), used to tend to her husband's date garden, outside Madinah, then carry the dates home in a basket on her head. She would also bring fodder and water to Zubayr's horse, and, after tending the crops and the horse, she would come back home and take care of the housework. Fâṭimah (⬥), the daughter of the Prophet (⬥), had hands that were chapped from her continual work in the house, and once asked her father to provide a slave or servant to help her, but he refused, saying that it was preferable for her to enjoy luxuries in the hereafter than to have them in this world.[6]

Some of the scholars point to such reports as evidence that women are expected to serve their husbands, whilst others suggest that their services were rendered voluntarily, and that this was a good deed on their part, for which they will be rewarded.

The Prophet (⬥) helped out around the house

Whatever the case, the fact that is most often overlooked (especially by some of our brothers!) is the fact that the Prophet (⬥) used to lend a hand in domestic tasks: in particular, he is known to have repaired his own shoes, stitched his own garments and milked his goat. He told the Companions, «The best among you are those who are best to their wives, and I am the best among you to my wives.» The general advice given in the Qur'an is:

(سورة النِّسَاء: ١٩)   ﴿ ... وَعَاشِرُوهُنَّ بِٱلْمَعْرُوفِ ... ۝ ﴾

❨... Live with them honourably on a footing of kindness and equity...❩   *(Qur'an 4: 19)*

It is suggested in particular that the husband should help as much as he can when his wife is ill, pregnant, or breastfeeding their child.[7]

Ramadan: a domestic treadmill?

Sadly, the issue of domestic drudgery raises its ugly head especially in Ramadan[8], where in many communities an undeclared cooking war breaks out, and each housewife fears that people on the *iftâr*[9] circuit are comparing notes, and that she will be judged and found wanting for the type, variety and quantity of food offered, the size and decor of her house, and so on. I remember when I embraced Islam, in the early 80s in Britain, Ramadan coincided with the longest days of the year, and the fast could be from 2 am until 9.30 pm. At that time, I met women who were exhausted from fasting, who were minding young children (which is exhausting enough in its own right), and who were also preparing *iftâr* and *suhoor*[10] for hordes of guests every day or every other day. Instead of being able to concentrate on worship, reading the Qur'an and praying *tarâweeh*,[11] these women were reduced to automata, cooking, cleaning up and cooking again throughout the holy month. It is slightly easier when Ramadan falls in the shorter days of the year, but the merry-go-round continues. One of these women later expressed her views quite clearly:

> Did you hear the one about the millionaire in Makkah? No, this is not a joke, it's all too true. This magnanimous gentleman opened his home during the holy month, and all and sundry were welcome to come and break their fast there each evening.

> Of course, the news spread like wildfire, and people came from all over Makkah to feast at the big man's table. When they got there, they found bread and cheese and jam. "Is that all?" they moaned. Where were the steaming mounds of rice, the rich stews and roast lamb? Where was the huge feast they had all hoped for?

> Then the man's wife spoke up. "Ramadan is the month of worship. If I were to spend the whole month preparing huge and elaborate feasts, when would I get the chance to pray *tarâweeḥ* and read the Qur'an?"

This lady has said what many of us feel. I have done it myself: got the kids off to school, started cooking at nine-thirty in the morning, and carried on cooking until ifṭâr, served the food, maybe managed to rush through *maghrib*[12] prayers, then spent the time from *'ishâ'*[13] until suḥoor clearing away the pots and pans, and preparing suḥoor for the men returning from tarâweeḥ prayers. By the time I have finished clearing away the second lot of pots and pans, it was *fajr*,[14] and then the whole cycle may start all over again!

What about the women's tarâweeḥ prayers? What about our reading and reciting the Qur'an? Many of us would be lucky to finish even one *juz*'[15] in the whole month, let alone read all thirty!

Yes, hospitality to guests is an important part of our faith and culture, but does it take precedence over our worship? Surely our forebears, the Companions, did not go in for such elaborate feasts each night in Ramadan. They lived simple and pious lives; guests were welcome to share whatever the family had, but I doubt that their womenfolk would have had to neglect their prayers in order to lay on a mega-spread for the visitors!

Ramadan seems to have become yet another excuse for excess and rivalry in worldly matters. Instead of trying to keep up with the Joneses (you know what I mean!) we should get things into perspective. Yes, we can cook pleasant food for our guest, but simple everyday fare is just as good as the fancy foods. Dare I suggest that other members of the family could lend a hand too! Then we women will have a chance to participate in the acts of worship which are the essence of Ramadan.[16]

The answer to this problem would, perhaps, be 'communal' iftârs in mosques or community centres, where families can either bring contributions to a 'pot-luck' iftâr or else donate money towards the cost of having a caterer prepare the food. This takes some of the pressure off women, and offers them the opportunity to stay and participate in the tarâweeḥ prayers too.

Babies, babies, babies!

Along with the image of the drudge comes the image of the Muslim woman who produces a baby every year. It is easy to have the impression that some Muslim women even think that fecundity is an article of faith, to the extent that there are those who ignore medical advice and continue to have more and more children, with the result that their health is ruined and they can hardly look after the children they already have. Less 'productive' sisters may (inadvertently or otherwise) be made to feel that there is something wrong with them, and they are committing some kind of sin of omission by not having hordes of children, although there may be sound medical or other reasons for their having only one or two children, or none at all.

Pointing this out does not mean that one is against women having large numbers of children. Some women are able to have huge families whilst keeping their health and sanity intact, and this is something to be admired and encouraged. However, those who do not enjoy such good health should not be made to feel pressured — whether by husbands, in-laws or the community — to produce more children. Sometimes women are made to feel this pressure even if they already have five or six children! Any woman who has produced so many children has certainly already helped to swell the ranks of the Ummah, but her priorities now should be to take care of her own health, and to nurture and educate her children soundly. There are also many other ways in which she can contribute to the community, according to her own interests and abilities.

Desperately seeking sons

Another issue is the quest for sons. Many Muslim men are so desperate for sons that they will keep on trying, regardless of the wife's feelings and health. The women may feel desperate too, if they feel that they will receive no recognition or esteem until they become mothers of sons, or fear that their husbands may divorce them or take second wives. Two, three or more daughters arrive, and the response is, "Better luck next time!" We need to remember that all children are a gift from Allah (ﷻ) and a trust from Him, and that He bestows what He (ﷺ) wills:

$$\text{﴿لِلَّهِ مُلْكُ ٱلسَّمَوَٰتِ وَٱلْأَرْضِ يَخْلُقُ مَا يَشَآءُ يَهَبُ لِمَن يَشَآءُ إِنَـٰثًا وَيَهَبُ}$$

$$\text{لِمَن يَشَآءُ ٱلذُّكُورَ ⑲ أَوْ يُزَوِّجُهُمْ ذُكْرَانًا وَإِنَـٰثًا وَيَجْعَلُ مَن يَشَآءُ عَقِيمًا}$$

$$\text{إِنَّهُ عَلِيمٌ قَدِيرٌ ⑳ ﴾}$$

(سورة الشّورىٰ: ٤٩-٥٠)

❴To Allah belongs the dominion of the heavens and the earth. He creates what He wills [and plans]. He bestows [children] male or female according to His Will [and Plan], or He bestows both males and females, and He leaves barren whom He will: for He is full of knowledge and power.❵   *(Qur'an 42: 49-50)*

Whatever the number or gender of children produced, the responsibility goes beyond providing food, clothing and shelter. Muslim parents have a duty to educate their children — girls as well as boys — and teach them Islam. The anti-girl bias was so widespread at the advent of Islam that, as is well-known, female infanticide was widespread. Combating such evils was a priority, and the Prophet (ﷺ) not only taught his followers to cherish and educate their daughters, but he also led by example. The prohibition on killing one's children was an integral part of Islam: people who came to declare their acceptance of Islam and to make their pledge of allegiance to the Prophet (ﷺ) had also to vow not to commit infanticide:

$$\text{﴿يَـٰٓأَيُّهَا ٱلنَّبِيُّ إِذَا جَآءَكَ ٱلْمُؤْمِنَـٰتُ يُبَايِعْنَكَ عَلَىٰٓ أَن لَّا يُشْرِكْنَ بِٱللَّهِ شَيْـًٔا وَلَا}$$

$$\text{يَسْرِقْنَ وَلَا يَزْنِينَ وَلَا يَقْتُلْنَ أَوْلَـٰدَهُنَّ وَلَا يَأْتِينَ بِبُهْتَـٰنٍ يَفْتَرِينَهُ بَيْنَ أَيْدِيهِنَّ}$$

$$\text{وَأَرْجُلِهِنَّ وَلَا يَعْصِينَكَ فِى مَعْرُوفٍ فَبَايِعْهُنَّ وَٱسْتَغْفِرْ لَهُنَّ ٱللَّهَ إِنَّ ٱللَّهَ غَفُورٌ}$$

$$\text{رَّحِيمٌ ⑫ ﴾}$$

(سورة المُمْتَحِنة: ١٢)

❴O Prophet! When believing women come to you to take the oath of fealty to you, that they will not associate in worship any thing whatever with Allah, that they will not steal, that they will not commit adultery [or fornication], that they will not kill their children, that they will not utter slander, intentionally forging falsehood, and that they will not disobey you in any just manner — then receive their fealty, and pray to Allah for the forgiveness [of their sins]: for Allah is Oft-Forgiving, Most Merciful.》

(Qur'an 60: 12)

Daughters are to be cherished

A number of hadiths indicate that daughters are to be cherished, educated and supported until they reach the age of maturity; the reward for doing this is no less than paradise.[17] In particular, the Messenger (ﷺ) said: «Whoever brings up two girls, so that they reach maturity, he and I shall enter paradise together (and he signalled this by placing two of his fingers together).»[18]

Perhaps the greatest proof of the attitude of the Prophet (ﷺ) towards girls is his own behaviour towards his daughters. He gave them love, was a dedicated and devoted father, and continued his concern for their well-being after they married.[19]

In fact, the changes brought by Islam in this regard were so revolutionary that a pagan poet made the satirical comment:

After the Prophethood of Muhammad,
there are girls and girls everywhere![20]

The education we provide for all of our children must equip them to live in the real world. For girls, this means more than 'home economics.'[21] For boys, this includes instilling a more practical attitude in them towards domestic tasks. Too many Muslim mothers have never taught their sons to wash their own plates, prepare their own food, make their own bed or iron their own clothes, which is why too many Muslim women today are over-burdened. Teaching sons to look after themselves will not only help those boys when they go out into the world on their own, but it will also make them better husbands and fathers in the future, *inshâ' Allâh*.

Nothing wrong with large families

Suggesting that Muslim women should not necessarily be automatic baby factories should not be taken to imply that Muslims should not have large families or that birth control should be the norm. There is a lot to be said for big families. The championship and support (moral and practical) that such families can find in their own ranks is a precious treasure that is to be valued and cherished. But each family must make its own decisions based on a number of factors, of which the wife's health and ability to cope should always be paramount, especially for Muslim families living in the West where the traditional support network of sisters, in-laws, aunts and cousins may well be lacking.

Birth control

Some couples may wish to 'space' their children, to allow the mother's body to recover from labour and birth before having another child. Other families may decide that they do not want to have any more children because of the mother's health. In such cases, most scholars indicate that contraception may be allowed as long as both husband and wife agree to it; but there is much debate as to the type of contraception to be used, and most modern 'methods' give rise to concerns. Therefore, Muslims need to be aware of what is involved so that they can make an informed decision.

The universal acceptable method according to Islam is *'azl* (coitus interruptus). Among the modern methods, particular caution is advised with regard to the IUD, or coil, which is in fact an early abortifacient (it allows conception to take place, but prevents implantation of the embryo) and may also cause heavy bleeding;[22] and the pill, which interferes with the natural cycles of the woman and has many side effects ranging from the unpleasant to the downright dangerous. Many non-Muslim women have also expressed concern about its prolonged use.[23] The 'morning-after pill' should be avoided by Muslim women too; if conception has taken place, this medication will kill the embryo. Barrier methods are less invasive, but may prove awkward or uncomfortable to use. Another option is the fertility awareness method, which is more scientifically accurate than the old rhythm method. These methods involve monitoring the menstrual cycle and determining which times of the month are 'safe periods', (that is, times when conception is less likely to occur). The fertility awareness method can also be used to determine when ovulation is likely to occur, for those wishing to conceive; but the rhythm method, unlike the fertility awareness method, is only suitable for those with regular menstrual cycles. Each couple must weigh the pros and cons and choose whatever suits them. There are no hard and fast rules; what suits one couple may not suit another.

Whilst considering a woman's domestic and maternal role, we must consciously and continually resist the negative Western image of this role. Islam gives this role a very high status, as is reflected in many hadiths.[24] We must continually remind ourselves to see it in this light, and promote the role of mother, whilst balancing it with due recognition of women's other needs, be they intellectual, social, economic, or whatever.

Interestingly enough, there is something of a similar movement already going on in the West, especially in North America, where "staying home instead" (which is the title of a book on the subject) is increasingly recognised as a valid option, and real women — the ones with husbands and children — are finally rebelling against the have-it-all attitude advocated by "childless career feminists".[25] An evocatively-titled book published by La Leche League, *The Heart Has Its Own Reasons*, describes these families as the "new pioneers" who are forging a new path, and a new lifestyle.[26] While they may look to the past for ideas on making do with less, or growing or making what they need, they are also very much part of the present, and thinking forward to the future with firm ideas on ecology, being 'green', home-schooling, and so on — which are also of interest to many Muslims.

Summary

Not every woman is cut out to be a domestic marvel. Some of us crave more intellectual stimulation than home and babies alone can provide. Others among us want nothing more than to channel all our creativity into making a home. In Islam, there is room for both types, although the emphasis has traditionally been on the domestic front. Housekeeping and baby producing, although important, are not pillars of faith. Husbands should lend a hand and even (dare I say it) expect and demand less, especially when the wife is ill, pregnant or breastfeeding, has hordes of tiny tots around her, or is working/studying outside the home. Muslims should also be less harsh towards one another, less demanding, and less critical. This will help to relieve some of the pressure on women and free them to concentrate on worship and learning more about Islam. Is this too much to ask?

CHAPTER FOUR

(Abuses of) Polygyny

$\mathscr{P}$olygyny has to be one of the greatest bug-bears around today, one that stalks even monogamous Muslims. The corny old stereotype of the 'sheikh' (usually pronounced 'sheek') or 'pasha' with the well-stocked harem is one that simply will not go away. From movies to novels to kids' cartoons, the 'Moslem' male with anything from two to two hundred wives is all too familiar.

Horror stories abound. Western journalists and researchers love to unearth cases of polygyny gone wrong. Then they can relate the tragic tales of neglected first wives, abandoned but un-divorced wives 'back home', and so on. Jan Goodwin[1] cites the extraordinary story of an American convert in the Middle East who is in her second polygynous marriage; in both cases, although the husband provided housing and food, he refused to tell the first wife of this second marriage, and his visits eventually became less and less frequent. The men were supposedly respectable persons, and one held an important position in an Islamic organisation. One cannot help agreeing with the suggestion that this was some kind of 'legalised mistress' set-up; the foreign wife may have had novelty value but there was no real intention of commitment. The whole agreement appears to be contrary to the spirit of Islam.

Goodwin also describes another case, that of a wife (this time one raised in Islam) who is resigned to the fact that her husband makes frequent trips to another Arab country where he will marry a girl, often from a poorer background, spend a few weeks with her, then divorce her. The first wife feels pity for the girls whose lives are ruined in this way (the unmarriageability of divorcees in Muslim cultures is notorious — and also contrary to the spirit of Islam), but she feels powerless to do anything about the situation.[2]

Of course, most Muslims are not partners in polygynous marriages, and perhaps such incidents are relatively rare, but they contain all the elements of a 'good human interest story', and so these, and not the many happy monogamous marriages, are what we hear so much about. There are many issues surrounding polygyny that need to be clarified.

Terminology

It should be pointed out here that the term 'polygamy', which is most commonly used to describe such marriages, in fact may apply to either a man having more than one wife or a woman having more than one husband. It has been pointed out that this word is too vague,[3] especially as Islamic polygamy is quite specific and is for men only: Muslim women are not allowed to have more than one husband at a time. More precise words relating to plural marriage are 'polygyny' (polygamy in which a man has more than one wife) and 'polyandry' (polygamy in which a woman has more than one husband). I will use the word 'polygyny' to refer to Islamic polygamy in this discussion. The Arabic term, by the way, is *ta'addud az-zawjât* (literally 'plurality of wives').

Polygyny is part of the Islamic set-up

Some Muslims attempt to explain polygyny away as strongly discouraged, because of the verse:

$$\ ...\ \text{فَإِنْ خِفْتُمْ أَلَّا تَعْدِلُوا فَوَاحِدَةً } ... \text{ ﴿٣﴾}$$ (سورة النِّسَاء : ٣)

❨If you fear that you will not be able to deal justly [with them], then [marry] only one...❩   *(Qur'an 4: 3)*

Subscribers to this opinion say that no man can ever be one hundred percent fair to two or more wives, so in effect the Qur'an is recommending monogamy. Those who favour plural marriages are equally passionate in defending and advocating the custom. We have to bear in mind the fact that Muslims must accept the undisputed teachings of their religion.

﴿وَمَا كَانَ لِمُؤْمِنٍ وَلَا مُؤْمِنَةٍ إِذَا قَضَى اللَّهُ وَرَسُولُهُ أَمْرًا أَن يَكُونَ لَهُمُ الْخِيَرَةُ مِنْ أَمْرِهِمْ ... ﴿٣٦﴾   (سورة الأحزَاب : ٣٦)

❨It is not befitting for a believer, man or woman, when a matter has been decided by Allah and His Messenger, to have any option about their decision...❩   *(Qur'an 33: 36)*

Whatever our own personal feelings and preferences (and many Muslim women honestly feel that they could not cope with their husband taking another wife), no Muslim can say that polygyny is not allowed. When we take into account the Qur'an, the practice of the Prophet (ﷺ) and his Companions, and the writings of Muslim scholars throughout history, we cannot get away from the fact that polygyny is allowed in Islam. Both monogamy and polygyny are acceptable within the social framework of Islam, and surely this is an indication of the universality of Islam, the religion that we are always proud of saying is the religion for all times and all places.

Polygyny as proof of Islamic universality

Monogamy is supposedly the norm in Western cultures (although in fact an enormous amount of hypocrisy exists), and Islam allows for this preference. A Muslim man who has one wife is doing nothing wrong. There are numerous parts of the Muslim world where the overwhelming majority of men have just one wife. Let us remember, however, that Islam is a religion for all times and all places. There are many situations that arise in which the advantages of having polygyny as an option are obvious. For one, there are and have been times and places in the history of human society where the number of females was greater than the number of males in a community. This is usually the case when war has ravaged a particular area. On an individual level, the option of polygyny can be a blessing. The 'surplus' of females would otherwise have to suffer the lack of male companionship and support, and would have no permissible outlet by which to satisfy their natural sexual desires. Without the option of polygyny, women who would otherwise love to be in a martial relationship would be forced to live a life of loneliness and celibacy, or they may end up in forbidden relationship just to satisfy their needs for attention, affection and sex.

Polygyny can be a blessing in more than one way. Take the actual case of a man whose wife of many years became mentally debilitated with a disease that no doctor was able to treat. The wife needed 24-hour care, and the husband was faced with the awful choice of either committing her to an institution, hiring full-time home care that he could afford, or divorcing her to render her a ward of the state (which of course he would not think of). This faithful Muslim husband instead married a second woman who became the devoted attendant of the first wife, taking full responsibility for bathing her, dressing her, spoon-feeding her, and giving her loving care and patient attention. At the same time, the husband was also able to satisfy his own natural desires and needs for companionship, affection and sex, and to give the second wife what she had been looking for — an attentive, caring spouse who could provide for her and who made her part of his family. The first wife eventually died of her illness, but she died in the loving arms of her co-wife, who along with the gentle devotion of the husband had made the quality of the last years of her life as good as it could be. This situation could only be resolved so compassionately through the legislation of polygyny, which is part of Allah's mercy to humanity.[4]

While Westerners tend to view monogamy as 'normal' and plural marriages as unthinkable, in many regions of the world, such as parts of Africa[5], polygyny is the norm, for complex socio-economic reasons; so in societies where Islam is spreading, converts need not fear that the new religion will require them to tear their families apart, or make the appalling and painful decision to keep just one wife, and divorce the rest. Islam is flexible enough to accommodate both styles of marriage. This is in direct contrast to the approach of missionaries in Africa, most of whom sought to impose a rigid European monogamy on their neophytes, which often led directly to a situation in which a woman who would — as a second wife in an Islamic polygynous marriage — have benefited from all the rights due to her, but instead has been forced (as a convert to Christianity) to choose between returning to a life of celibacy as a single woman or living in an adulterous relationship as her ex-husband's mistress!

Western hypocrisy

The supposed monogamy of Western cultures, however, is nothing more than a species of hypocrisy, in many instances. Although Christianity preaches 'one man, one wife', many nominally-Christian men are, in effect, polygynous. The 'other woman', 'mistress' or 'bit on the side' is an all too familiar figure in the popular mind. Historically, in England, it has always been taken for granted that anyone from the king downwards might have a 'kept woman'. Bigamists — such as the character who had a wife and kids on each side of the river that flowed through his city, all of whom showed up at his funeral and fought for the role of grieving family[6] — are at the very least regarded as eccentric, but more usually are roundly condemned in literature and newspapers (not to mention being liable to punishment by law), whilst people turn a blind eye to illicit affairs with mistresses. No one ever expresses much concern for the wife and legitimate children, who may be devastated when they learn of the unsavoury antics of the husband and father, and all too often have to bear the shame and humiliation in silence.

Islam, as has been pointed out by many writers, takes hold of the natural urges of human beings, which Allah has created in us for a reason, and limits and channels those energies, setting up safeguards and seeking to preserve the best interests of individuals and of society as a whole.

Fairness (*'adl*) in plural marriages

In the case of polygyny, the natural urge of some men to have more than one partner is controlled, and boundaries are set that will allow the man to enjoy more than one relationship without shirking his duties towards each wife and any children that may be born. This urge is thus limited and controlled: a maximum number of wives is set, and there are clear conditions for polygyny. The man should have sufficient financial resources to support a second family, and he should be able and willing to treat both wives equally with regard to all rights given to them by Islam. If he is unable to comply with these conditions, then he should not take a second (or subsequent) wife. Furthermore, strict guidelines are set out by Muslim scholars regarding the time to be spent with each wife, and the provision of food, clothing, shelter, and so forth. These may be outlined as follows:[7]

Time: The husband with two or more wives is obliged to divide his time equally between his wives; a new wife may have three or seven days in a row, as a kind of honeymoon, then the division of time starts equally between the wives. The husband is obliged to include in this rota wives who may be menstruating, bleeding following childbirth, post-menopausal, or ill — including mental illness. This should make it abundantly clear that polygyny is not just about physical pleasures (contrary to popular notions). The scholars emphasise the wives' human need for companionship and support; as regards the conjugal relationship, they remind us that both husband and wife have an equal and mutual right to satisfaction, but the details of the intimate relationship are something to be kept private, and this is one area that is not for discussion among co-wives or with anybody else.

Travel: If the husband is travelling and can only take one wife with him, he is not allowed to play favourites. He must use an impartial way of deciding who is to accompany him, such as casting lots, which is the way the Prophet (ﷺ) made such decisions.

<u>Gifts</u>: If the husband chooses to buy a gift for one wife, he should give a gift to all his wives, but the gifts need not be identical as tastes and preferences differ. He may give the other wife or wives the monetary value of the gift, or another gift of equivalent value.

<u>Spending</u>: The husband is obliged to provide at least the basics for each wife, according to his means, local conditions, and so on. However, the spending need not be identical in each case. Philips and Jones give the example of one wife's refrigerator breaking down whilst the second wife's fridge is working perfectly well; so money would be spent for the first wife but not, in this case, for the second. Another example is one wife being of a larger size than another, in which case her clothes would necessarily cost more.

<u>Children</u>: The rights of children are considered independently of their mothers. A wife with, say, six children will obviously require larger accommodation and expenditure than a wife with two or no children. As the husband may easily find himself spending more time in the home of a wife with children than one with no children, it is suggested that he take the children out to parks, for example, or else take them to the home of the wife to whom his time is allotted, if this is possible. (In some plural marriages this is not a problem at all; in others, human nature being what it is, it would cause more problems than it would solve. Each case is unique and the partners involved must make their own decisions.)

Common sense and maturity

All Muslims are supposed to have a commonsense and mature attitude towards life, but these qualities are extra important to partners in plural marriages. The husband has a responsibility to be fair, but his wives also have a responsibility not to make his life a misery. If the co-wives get along well, then all well and good; but if they do not, they should not be forced to spend time together and 'make friends'. A co-wife writing in *Islamic Sisters International* describes that apart from their husband, she and his other wife have nothing in common: their interests, tastes and personalities are so different that it is better for all concerned that they keep a distance from one another.[8] It is also unfair and immature to use one's own children (or those of a co-wife) as pawns in whatever rivalries may exist — leave the children out of it!

The great welfare polygyny scam

Sadly, there are, of course, unpleasant realities in polygyny that occur when Islamic injunctions are not heeded. One of the more dubious practices surrounding plural marriage, referred to by Bilal Philips and Jameelah Jones,[9] is what may be described as the great welfare polygyny scam. Perhaps more common in North America, but not unknown in other Western welfare states, this is the scenario in which a man may have two or more wives, and puts them both on welfare. They may live in government-provided housing, and they may even be claiming welfare as 'single mothers' if the marriages have not been registered with the state! This scam takes one's breath away; the lying and deceit alone are not characteristics one would hope to find in Muslims. Additionally, this practice is contrary to the rulings of the scholars, that the would-be polygynous husband should be able to provide for a second family. It also raises issues of what kind of an image of Islam is presented by such goings-on; do we really need to add anything else to the already-heavy burden of negative stereotypes we must bear every day? Bilal Philips and Jameelah Jones are quite scathing in their condemnation of such goings-on:

The receipt of welfare checks by married women, especially in the case of plural marriages, involves lies and deceit, which are among the most despicable traits that a Muslim may possess. Any man who marries a woman in order to control her welfare check is without doubt a base and vile creature who should be ashamed to eat the food which belongs to her helpless children.[10]

These writers hint that many of these practitioners of welfare-polygyny are those who "over-emphasise outward things like eastern dress" and "claim that they cannot work for the *kâfirs*"[11] — but they are not above living on hand-outs from those same "kâfirs"! This is clearly indicative of an extremely lopsided view of Islam, marriage and responsibility. One cannot help wondering why, if dealing with or working for "kâfirs" is so abhorrent to these people, they do not emigrate to a Muslim country? (The answer, perhaps: no welfare cheques).

Convert wives rejected

Muslim women have also voiced their objections to men who take a wife from different ethnic, linguistic, or cultural background — often a convert to Islam, then subsequently take another wife of their own background. This can be extremely hurtful, as if the first wife was "never the real thing". It is even worse if the first wife is then divorced and loses her children, to be raised by the husband and the second wife. A British-born convert who married a Middle-Eastern man endured years of abuse, then was informed by her husband that he was going to take a "more appropriate" second wife, that is, a young girl from back home. This young bride was to be installed in the family home to raise the children of the first wife, who was to be shunted off to a small apartment to live alone, yet not to be divorced. This sister was able to 'escape' with her children and start a better life elsewhere,[12] but others are not so fortunate.

Although these horror stories exist, and one fears that they may represent only the tip of the iceberg, the fact remains that most Muslim men have only one wife, and some would say that is more than enough! Especially in this day and age, when housing and food and clothing, all things that the husband is required by Islam to provide for his wife or wives and children, are so expensive.

Polygyny as a threat

Another issue is the use of polygyny as a threat. Some men will warn their wives, "If you do not (do what I say), I'll take another wife!" Although some scholars suggest that this may be permitted in cases where the wife is neglecting her duties and this is leading to unacceptable tension and an unpleasant atmosphere within the household,[13] it is not a threat to be used lightly or repeated *ad nauseam*. Husbands should not be so quick to accuse their wives of neglecting their duties, especially when the wife may have a job or studies outside the home, and/or be pregnant/ breastfeeding and/or be caring for little ones with none of the traditional extended-family support that may exist back home. In fact, issuing such threats carelessly may well have a negative effect. Witness the plea made by an American sister:

> ... husbands who use the right to have additional wives as a threat to force their will on their wife destroys the love and respect she had for him earlier in their marriage.[14]

It is also worth remembering that the Prophet (ﷺ) advised a husband to: «Feed her when you feed yourself, clothe her when you clothe yourself, do not strike her on the face, do not use hurtful language to her (*lâ tuqabbiḥ*), and do not leave her except in the home.»

The expression *lâ tuqabbiḥ* was explained by the scholar al-Mundhiri as meaning, "Do not say things which will displease her or hurt her, and do not say things like, May Allah make you experience bad things."[15] The Prophet (ﷺ) advised husbands to treat their wives with compassion, not to issue threats.

Can a wife stipulate in the marriage contract that the husband may not take another wife?

Another question is whether a wife can insert a condition in the marriage contract preventing her husband from taking another wife. There are two opinions among the scholars: one is that a marriage contract should not ban any practice that is allowed in Islam; another view is that the woman is allowed to state terms that protect her rights, including living in her own locality, and stopping her husband from taking another wife.[16]

The green-eyed monster

Jealousy is another issue that is raised when polygyny is discussed. It is a part of human nature, hence the strict rules about time, provisions, and so forth are to be implemented. The Prophet (ﷺ) is known to have loved one wife, 'Â'ishah (﵂), more than the others, but he still made the effort to treat all of his wives equally in the things he had control over, and prayed to Allah that he not be judged for what he could not control.[17] The only just thing to do in a situation where a husband is fonder of one wife than the other(s) is not to make it too obvious, and not to hurt the feelings of the wife who is 'less favoured'.

The positive side of polygyny

Despite all the negative images and horror stories, polygyny can work. I have met sisters who enjoy their 'free time' when the husband is with his other family; they use this time to socialise with other sisters, host or attend study circles, study, read, sew, and so on. Maryam Jemeelah is known to have chosen to be a second wife so that she would be able to continue to study and write.[18] In an ideal situation, the wives can be friends, providing an inbuilt support system whereby they can help with the kids when one wife is sick, and so on.[19] In one unique and remarkable case, a tearaway American teenager was taken back home by a Saudi business associate and close friend of her father to be 'mothered' by his three wives with no strings attached; she calmed down, grew up and eventually joined the family as the fourth wife.[20]

Summary

There are many abuses of polygyny, sadly, which may account for much of the opposition to this practice among Muslims. However, we cannot get away from the fact that polygyny is allowed in Islam, and in some cultures at some times this is a positive advantage. Although it is widely viewed as a 'bad thing', there are circumstances in which polygyny may be the lesser of two evils, and in some situations it may even be positively beneficial. As for example, a case in which one wife is suffering from ill-health and the other wife is able to be a supportive friend.

Those who do abuse polygyny will have to answer to Allah for their deeds, just as those who abuse other rights will. When polygyny is embarked upon in a true Islamic spirit, with the intention of pleasing Allah and with an awareness of one's Islamic responsibilities, then it can be a successful and satisfying venture for all concerned. Whilst many Muslims will never be partners in polygynous marriages, we should not condemn out of hand those who choose to be, or regard them as 'strange', so long as their conduct remains within Islamic limits.

CHAPTER FIVE

Domestic Violence

$\mathcal{D}$omestic violence, spousal abuse, battered wives... Whatever label you want to apply, violence against women (and children) exists in all societies and classes, and the Muslim world is far from immune. On bad days, one might be forgiven for thinking that in-home violence is particularly endemic to the Muslim community', and families where there is no such violence may wonder, with some sense of relief, how they managed to stay the course of gentleness and effect the peaceful resolution of their own conflicts.

Anyone who spends enough time with Muslim women will most likely eventually hear some tales of woe, whether second or third-hand, or directly from the sisters concerned, who may even show the bruises and injuries received. In recent years, more and more information is coming to light. The Muslim Women's Helpline (MWHL) of London, England, founded in 1989, has reported numerous cases where it has helped Muslim women who are facing domestic violence. The US Muslim women's magazine *Islamic Sisters International* has devoted an entire issue to the matter of spousal abuse; they checked the authenticity of the letters and reports they received, and tried to help where they could. In many cases, the local Muslim community leadership was far from helpful, blaming the women themselves and pressuring them to stay put (of which more later).

What happens to battered wives?

The details of domestic violence are horrific. Some women undergo years of torment at the hands of their husbands. The abuse may be physical or mental — often both. Slaps, punches and kicks are commonplace. Husbands may resort to using weapons, such as knives, or the wife may suffer burns.[1] The MWHL reports one case where a woman came to their office with stitches in her head from the most recent assault.[2] It comes as no surprise to learn that hospitalisation is not uncommon.[3]

Mental or emotional abuse is also widespread, with or without physical assaults. If anything, it is more insidious than the beatings. The husband may continually insult his wife, calling her worthless, ugly, fat, stupid, dumb, lazy, and so forth. It may occur alongside the beating, or without any overt violence. Such name-calling on a persistent basis wears away any person's self-esteem to a level where they can barely function. Threats to take a second wife, and/or remove the children and ship them back to the husband's family or country may also be used.[4]

Some of the issues are particularly pertinent to convert wives. Some such women have found that their husbands who were raised as Muslims may begin to regard them as "not quite good enough"[5]. There have even been instances where a man raised as a Muslim, having recently re-committed himself to his religion, begins to view his Western wife (converted or otherwise), whom he may have met in a not-very-Islamic way, as somehow inferior and unworthy, despite the fact that she may be the mother of his children and may be willing and eager to raise them as Muslims. This new-found contempt may also translate into physical, verbal or mental cruelty.

Does wife-beating have Qur'anic sanction?

The domestic violence issue is further complicated by interpretations and translations of the Qur'an that appear to indicate that 'wife-beating' is sanctioned in Soorat an-Nisâ' (4: 34). This, of course, is a reference that is pounced upon by certain feminists, orientalists, journalists and anyone else who wants to portray Islam in the worst possible light. Sadly, the behaviour of many Muslims does nothing to dispel such dismal stereotypes. The verse in question follows the verse about qawwâmah discussed in chapter one:

﴿ٱلرِّجَالُ قَوَّٰمُونَ عَلَى ٱلنِّسَآءِ بِمَا فَضَّلَ ٱللَّهُ بَعْضَهُمْ عَلَىٰ بَعْضٍ وَبِمَآ أَنفَقُواْ مِنْ أَمْوَٰلِهِمْ فَٱلصَّٰلِحَٰتُ قَٰنِتَٰتٌ حَٰفِظَٰتٌ لِّلْغَيْبِ بِمَا حَفِظَ ٱللَّهُ وَٱلَّٰتِي تَخَافُونَ نُشُوزَهُنَّ فَعِظُوهُنَّ وَٱهْجُرُوهُنَّ فِي ٱلْمَضَاجِعِ وَٱضْرِبُوهُنَّ فَإِنْ أَطَعْنَكُمْ فَلَا تَبْغُواْ عَلَيْهِنَّ سَبِيلًا إِنَّ ٱللَّهَ كَانَ عَلِيًّا كَبِيرًا ۝ وَإِنْ خِفْتُمْ شِقَاقَ بَيْنِهِمَا فَٱبْعَثُواْ حَكَمًا مِّنْ أَهْلِهِ وَحَكَمًا مِّنْ أَهْلِهَآ إِن يُرِيدَآ إِصْلَٰحًا يُوَفِّقِ ٱللَّهُ بَيْنَهُمَآ إِنَّ ٱللَّهَ كَانَ عَلِيمًا خَبِيرًا ۝ ﴾

(سورة النِّساء: ٣٤-٣٥)

◆Men are the protectors and maintainers of women, because Allah has given the one more [strength] than the other, and because they support them from their means. Therefore the righteous women are devoutly obedient, and guard in [the husband's] absence what Allah would have them guard. As to those women on whose part you fear disloyalty and ill-conduct [*nushooz*], admonish them [first], [next], refuse to share their beds, [and last] beat them [lightly] [*aḍribuhunna*]; but if they return to obedience, seek not against them means [of annoyance]: for Allah is Most High, Great [above you all]. If you fear a breach between the two of them, appoint [two] arbiters, one from his family and the others from hers; if they wish for peace, Allah will cause their reconciliation: for Allah has full knowledge and is acquainted with all things.》

(Qur'an 4: 34-35)

This is Yusuf 'Ali's translation, in which the Arabic word *aḍribuhunna* is rendered as "beat them (lightly)". Marmaduke Pickthall, on the other hand, translates the same word as 'scourge', an altogether stronger word. When Western feminists and others with an axe to grind (but with little or no knowledge of Arabic) read a translation of the Qur'an, they seize upon this emotive word as proof that Islam oppresses women. The Arabic word *ḍaraba* means to beat, strike or hit; the English dictionary tells us that 'scourge' means to whip, chastise, afflict, oppress, or harass! Amina Wadud-Muhsin points out that ḍaraba ('first form', for readers familiar with the Western methods of teaching Arabic grammar) does not necessarily imply force or violence, and contrasts it with the intensive second form *ḍarraba*, which means 'to strike repeatedly or intensely'. It is the first form that is used in this verse.[6] In fact, as the English word 'beating' has the meaning of hitting repeatedly, it should also be avoided.

A last resort in specific circumstances

The verse quoted above, far from suggesting that wife battering should be a way of life, refers to one particular situation: namely the fear of *nushooz* on the part of the wife. *Nushooz* is variously interpreted as defiance, arrogance, rebellion, disobedience, open lewdness and obscenity, infidelity or adultery. Such attitudes and behaviours are, of course, forbidden to all Muslims, male and female alike; but even in the extreme case of the wife's misconduct, a light 'rap on the wrist' is regarded as the **last resort**. The verse outlines a series of steps to be taken: first of all the husband should admonish his wife, giving her the chance to realise the error of her ways and to put things right. There may even have been a misunderstanding, that may then be cleared up. The next step is to withhold marital relations, which again will provide space for both partners to think things through and to put right what they can. If the wife is still stubborn and defiant, then disciplining her physically (*daraba*) is the final measure. However, it is clear that the physical punishment is to be so light as to be a mere token; men are cautioned against using a stick or other instrument, and against striking the head or the face.[7] Men who seek to emulate the Prophet (ﷺ) should remember that he never struck another person, except on the battlefield.

Hadiths on corporal punishment

This issue is so important that it is worth quoting some hadiths on the matter. That the Prophet (ﷺ) was opposed to the abuse of women is clear from hadiths such as the following:

«Do not strike your wife as if she were a slave. Would you strike her and then at the end of the day sleep with her?»[8]

«It was reported to the Prophet (ﷺ) that some of the Companions struck their wives, whereupon he said: Certainly those are not the best among you.»[9]

«'Ā'ishah (ؓ) narrated that the Messenger (ﷺ) never struck a woman or a servant with his hand. He only raised his hand in jihad for Allah's cause.»[10]

Historical context

It is worth noting the background against which verse 35 of Soorat an-Nisâ' was revealed. As Aminah Wadud-Muhsin points out, Arabian society at the advent of Islam was a society in which appalling violence towards women was commonplace (witness female infanticide, for example). Far from giving permission for wife-beating, this verse may be viewed as prohibiting violence against women.[11]

Wife-beating in the guise of 'correction'

Back to the real world, far removed from Islamic ideals, we find that wife-beating in the guise of sanctioned punishment occurs for any number of reasons, many of them trivial. Many Muslim women have large families; having more than three children, often born close together, is not uncommon, and — in many cases in the West — they do not have the traditional extended family support of sisters, aunts, cousins, and so forth. Being solely responsible for house and children, perhaps with a husband who is working or studying long hours, and perhaps living in an isolated setting where there are few other Muslim women to mix with and make friends, can at times be an unbearable burden for any woman. However, anything less than perfect housekeeping or cooking is a common excuse for wife-beating. One male Muslim writer suggests that failure to wear "fineries" for the husband when he wants it would be just cause for a husband to administer a beating.[12] This is an appalling idea. Many busy mothers of small children may simply feel so exhausted that "fineries" would be the last thing on their minds.

Causes of nushooz

Another male writer, Rahman, lists a number of possible causes of nushooz and suggests that husbands should avoid letting these happen.[13] The list includes boredom and loneliness; and what woman can say that she has never felt bored and lonely at home all day with small children and severely limited access to intelligent, adult conversation? But Rahman's recommended solution to boredom and loneliness includes the use of TV and radio, and encouraging wives to spend some time shopping in department stores! These suggestions are not particularly Islamic, to say the least. I would suggest that encouraging women to enrol in a course of study, to do voluntary work, and/or to mix and make friends with other Muslim women of decent character would be far more positive solutions to those problems.

Who can abused wives turn to?

So, to whom can these women turn when they are caught up in domestic violence? Women who have been raised in Islam and have Muslim relatives may be able to turn to their families for help, and their fathers or brothers may be able to intervene. This is along the lines of the recommendation in Soorat an-Nisâ' (4: 35). However, not all women are so fortunate; there are those whose families may not be supportive, or there may be tremendous pressure stemming from traditional cultural concerns. A great stigma is attached to divorce, and the family may be seen to 'lose face' if the daughter's marriage fails. The plight of the convert woman may be even worse; most converts do not have the family support to back them up, and even the most concerned of non-Muslim families will find it hard, if not impossible, to get involved in 'Islamic' disputes and procedures surrounding marital strife. There is also the ever-present possibility of being met with the attitude (spoken or unspoken) that says, "I told you so," and "What do you expect? He is a foreigner and Islam is foreign."

Some women try to turn to the local mosque or Islamic centre for help, but sadly no help may be forthcoming. Too many mosques are notoriously male-only bastions where women's presence is barely tolerated. How, then, can any woman in need get help? I am reminded of an occasion in the early 90s when two white women in Western dress came to the door of a small-town, men-only mosque in Britain. Most of the men present were almost apoplectic at the sight of unveiled females in the mosque, and wanted them to either cover up or, preferably. go away. Finally one brother decided to speak to them politely and at least give them a chance to say why they were there. It turned out that they were Bosnian refugees seeking charity and help from their brothers in Islam. This incident is just one example of how difficult it is for women to approach local mosques in many areas.

A poor track record

It is known that certain individuals and certain organisations are frequently a source of great help and comfort to sisters in distress, but there are too many others that have a poor track record in helping vulnerable sisters. Too many accounts describe male leaders of the community laughing off the women's cries for help, and/or siding automatically with the men. Some even quote (or misquote) verses and hadiths to make the woman feel guilty for complaining, and thus send her back to endure more of the same, — almost as a kind of living martyrdom![14]

Convert women may be in an even worse situation. All too often, there is a feeling that they are not being taken seriously.

One documented case describes an English Muslim woman who endured a "hellish" 11-year marriage followed by an "even more traumatic divorce". This lady points out that whilst many Muslims are welcoming and willingly teach a newcomer about prayer and fasting, their support fades quickly when troubles come along:

> ... when faced with real life problems they [those raised as Muslims] do not want to know. After six months of trying to seek advice about my problems, during which time I spoke with six different authorities on Islam from various mosques, I was finally told, "You are English, go to your own law, we cannot help you."[15]

And what happens when Western convert women "go to their own law", or when any Muslim woman in distress finds no other option than to throw herself on the mercy of the system of the country in which she lives? In all Western countries, even those with a better track record on multiculturalism and tolerance, she runs the risk of being misunderstood, being placed in precarious and Islamically unacceptable situations, and even of being pressured to reject her culture and religion. Ironically, Western converts who may have faced discrimination within the Muslim community for being Western may now find themselves facing discrimination for being Muslim.

Women's refuges

Many Western countries now have women's refuges: 'safe houses' where battered women and children can escape domestic violence and find some kind of respite whilst they decide what to do next. Counselling and help to find housing, welfare, and so on, are also available to women in these refuges. The addresses of such places are kept secret, for the protection of the women; this is because many abusive husbands will pursue their wives and seek to attack them again. Refuges have strict rules about opening the door and answering the phone, and it is guaranteed to be a man-free zone. There are also rules restricting or banning drugs and alcohol.[16]

Whilst the idea of the refuges, in theory, is excellent, there are problems in reality, especially for Muslim women finding themselves in such places. There will be a cross-section of women present, many of whom may have lifestyles vastly different from those of Muslim women. Apart from dietary considerations and the problems of communal cooking facilities, apparently simple things like the manner of speech may pose difficulties; some women may be used to swearing frequently, which would be offensive to most Muslim women. One Muslim woman who had to spend time in a refuge, sent there by social services, found the experience horrific: the other families there "behaved like animals".[17]

Furthermore, given the level of Western ignorance and stereotyping of Islam, many refuge workers may not be familiar with or sympathetic towards Islam or organised religion in general. (There is clearly great scope for Islamic organisations to contact and inform such agencies of the cultural needs of Muslims.) The current trend is to be — or at least to say that one is — accepting of all cultures and lifestyle choices; but I have found that in many cases, the line is drawn at encountering women who willingly cover themselves and follow Islam. A few years ago I met some refuge workers who insisted that they would be accepting of all cultures, including women who choose to wear the hijab (I seized the opportunity to make the point that many women wear the hijab by choice; it is not imposed by their menfolk); but the fact remains that there are others who would pressure a vulnerable Muslim woman into removing her hijab. This has actually happened in some cases.[18] However, a woman in need, who may have to flee for her own safety, will not be in a position to 'shop around' for the best refuge.

One answer may be for Muslims themselves to set up refuges, and attempts have been made in some areas. In a case that sadly demonstrates the lack of understanding of the sensitivity of this issue, one organisation that wanted to set up a refuge and had even purchased a building, also published photographs of it and gave the name of the small town in which it was located! How could any woman feel safe going there? An enraged husband might be determined enough to track her down and cause trouble, not only to his wife, but to the other women, children and workers in the building. It is clear that much work remains to be done on this front.

What if the husband is guilty of nushooz?

Another important question that arises is: what if it is the husband who is guilty of nushooz? Sometimes a decent, sincerely devout woman finds herself married to a man who is the opposite. This may be an arranged marriage that has been forced on such a woman, or the man may have been deceiving the woman and her family or guardian. Often men who are guilty of nushooz are also abusive to their wives, oppressing them and restricting their freedom whilst expecting to get away scot-free with whatever escapades they can. However bad the situation, the woman in such cases has no Islamic sanction to retaliate with corporal punishment. Indeed, that would solve nothing. Scholars say that she should be able to go to family members or community leaders for help. This may be a somewhat idealistic — or even unrealistic — suggestion in light of the experiences referred to above.

Another option is to ask for a divorce (khul'). The Qur'an forbids men to keep women in order to torment them; they should be kept in kindness or released in kindness:

﴾وَإِذَا طَلَّقْتُمُ ٱلنِّسَاءَ فَبَلَغْنَ أَجَلَهُنَّ فَأَمْسِكُوهُنَّ بِمَعْرُوفٍ أَوْ سَرِّحُوهُنَّ بِمَعْرُوفٍ وَلَا تُمْسِكُوهُنَّ ضِرَارًا لِتَعْتَدُوا وَمَن يَفْعَلْ ذَلِكَ فَقَدْ ظَلَمَ نَفْسَهُ ... ﴿٢٣١﴾﴾

(سورة البَقَرَة: ٢٣١)

﴾When you divorce women, and they fulfil the term [of their 'iddah], either take them back on equitable terms or set them free on equitable terms; but do not take them back to injure them, [or] to take undue advantage; if any one does that, he wrongs his own soul...﴿   *(Qur'an 2: 231)*

Sadly, most cultures attach a great stigma to divorce, with the result that many women will do almost anything to avoid it. But it has to be said that there is no virtue in remaining under oppression; Islam has provided a way out in such situations.

Persistent offenders would do well to remember the authentic hadith: «Beware the curse of the oppressed, for there is no screen between their supplication and Allah.»[19]

Roots of violence

What are the causes of this widespread domestic violence? When we look for reasons, we find a vicious circle. The roots lie in childhood: unequal treatment of boys and girls is common in many Muslim cultures. It may take the form of better food and education for boys, or allowing boys more 'freedom', so they grow up with the idea that they can do anything they want. I have seen Muslim families where the women are on 24-hour call to cook meals from scratch when the men demand to be fed, or to do every single menial domestic chore. Small children soon get the idea, and a woman with more egalitarian views, but an 'old-fashioned' husband, will have a hard time teaching her sons to cook or clean. They will have already learned, from example, that this is 'women's work'.

I have even seen Muslim fathers forbid their wives to restrain or chastise a one-year-old boy who is 'into everything', even when his antics cause great inconvenience (such as emptying flour out all over the kitchen floor) or danger to himself (sticking things into electrical sockets). This is bad enough, but many children are also growing up with regular exposure to domestic violence, and will see it as 'normal'. In one case, an eight-year-old boy came home from a lousy day at school and slapped his younger sister. When the mother intervened, the boy told her that he was just doing what he saw his father do; if he had a bad day at work he would come home and take it out on his wife. Even worse, the father approved of what his son had done, and administered another beating to his wife for daring to say that she disagreed with him.[20]

Breaking the cycle

How can we break the cycle of violence? As always, we have to go back to the Qur'an and the Sunnah. We have already looked at the one verse that refers to corporal punishment; we should also remind ourselves of what the Prophet (ﷺ) had to say on the matter:

«"Do not strike your wife as if she were a slave. Would you strike her and then at the end of the day sleep with her?»[21]

«Let no Muslim man consider a Muslim woman as his enemy. If you do not like one of her ways, you will like another.»[22]

«'Â'ishah (ﷺ) narrated that the Messenger (ﷺ) never struck a woman or a servant with his hand. He only raised his hand in jihad for Allah's cause.»[23]

In fact, we can understand from the words of the Prophet (ﷺ) that using corporal punishment is unlikely to achieve the desired results; repeated physical force, whether designed to 'correct' or abuse, can do nothing but arouse hatred and a desire for revenge — feelings that are antithetical to the Islamic ideal of marriage.[24] The Prophet (ﷺ) said: «A woman is like a rib which will break if you try to straighten it. You can benefit from it even if it remains bent as it was made»[25]. [26]

Describing a woman as being like a rib is not derogatory, as some feminists might have us believe; this hadith is an example of the wisdom and understanding displayed by the Prophet (ﷺ), who understood the nature of women and taught his followers to respect and cherish them.

So, to break the vicious cycle requires adherence to the Qur'an and the Sunnah; it means that the emulation of the Prophet (ﷺ) has to go beyond growing a beard, wearing a certain style of clothing and eating with only three fingers of the right hand. The Prophet (ﷺ) used to help out with domestic chores, and he never hit women, children, or servants — even though he lived at a time when such violent acts were commonplace. The burden is on our brothers to change their attitudes and actions; parents, too, have a duty to educate their sons to respect girls and women, and to be their protectors, rather than their abusers.

Summary

Domestic violence does not have any religious sanction. The one and only reference in the Qur'an that allows a man to impose corporal punishment on his wife applies to specific circumstances, and prescribes a symbolic 'slap on the wrist' as a form of correction, and only as the last resort. Given the proverbial jealousy of the Eastern male, remarkable restraint is being demanded of the Muslim husband who fears indiscretion on his wife's part! Islamic teaching, and the example of the Prophet (ﷺ), show us that violence has no place in a Muslim home, which should be a place filled with love, tranquillity and co-operation between family members.

CHAPTER SIX

Abuse of Non-Muslim Women

*T*he sisters on the bus felt uncomfortable. The family group had been staring at them all the way out of town. As the bus trundled through the English countryside, they could feel that they were being watched, although every time the Muslim women glanced at the mother and grandmother, they quickly looked away. They were used to stares. In the West, women wearing the hijab (especially, perhaps, white Muslim women) still find themselves the subject of this kind of unwelcome attention. Meanwhile, the sisters themselves stole a few surreptitious glances of their own: the curly-headed toddler on the younger woman's lap did not look like the average white English youngster. There was something about him...

Towards the end of the journey, the mother and daughter finally plucked up the courage to approach the sisters. Their stares had not been intended to be rude; they had never seen English Muslims before, and had wanted to speak to them, but felt too shy. The story came out, and the mystery of the toddler's appearance was resolved. His mother had had a relationship with a foreign student, a Muslim who had been attending a nearby university, and the child was the result. The father had not cared about the fact that he had had a child, and had returned to his homeland. The young woman was left to raise the child alone, and felt that she should teach the child something about his father's country and religion, but did not have a clue where to begin. She knew very little about Islam, but at least was able to recognise the hijab-wearing sisters as having something to do with her child's father's background.

Then there was the Arab sister, newly arrived in the West to study, who met a convert sister and had a lengthy conversation about all sorts of things. One of the issues that came up was the moral attitude in the West. Like many Easterners, this woman thought that all Western girls were 'easy'. She was very surprised, but pleasantly so, to learn that this is not at all the case. When I was in high school, there were many of us who had high moral standards and chose not to follow many of the ways of our peers. Some of us had religious reasons for doing so, but that was not always the case. I met plenty of people who did not drink, smoke, do drugs or 'fool around' for reasons of health or plain common sense. We had to endure a lot of ridicule from those who thought we were 'nerds' and 'prudes', but looking back, that was a small price to pay for retaining our self-respect!

Taking advantage of non-Muslims is not 'OK'

Unfortunately, the notion that Western woman are 'easy' and just there to be taken advantage of is all too common among Muslims. To some extent, it is an extension of the mistaken and decidedly un-Islamic notion that it is acceptable for non-Muslims to be deceived, cheated and fleeced in business and other dealings (of which more later). Some Muslims seem to feel that there is some kind of religious sanction for such behaviour, or at least have the notion that they will not be questioned or punished because the other person is not Muslim, so it does not really matter. There are claims that some religions do indeed sanction, if not encourage, such treatment of those who are not of their faith. I have no desire to engage in inter-faith mud-slinging by elaborating further. The point is that Islam is not of that ilk, and Muslims have no grounds whatsoever for abusing those who are not of their faith.

All fornication is forbidden

What Islam has to say about fornication is that it is forbidden, regardless of whether the partners are Muslims or not (in fact, fornication is also forbidden by Judaism and Christianity, at least in their historical forms). Although popular thinking tends to put the blame on the female — the infamous double standard — Islam recognises that it takes two, and both partners are held equally responsible. Remember: the injunction to lower one's gaze and guard one's chastity is addressed to men as well as women, and in fact men are cautioned first.

The problem is that temptation is all around, especially in Western societies. Standards have changed (in other words, slipped), so that what was unacceptable a generation ago is now commonplace, and things that were shameful and hidden are now flaunted openly and even applauded by others. It is well known that young Muslim men, coming from more conservative societies, may be 'freaked out' by what they see when they come to the West, and many of them jump head-first into the mire. It is very difficult for them to resist the temptations, which is where Islamic *tarbiyah* [1] comes in. Instead of ignoring what is going on and hoping that it will go away, or at least pass us by, we should take matters into our own hands, be realistic about the world we live in, and equip our young people to cope with the very real pressures of life in the West.

Marriage to women of the People of the Book

Many Muslims believe that as Islam allows Muslim men to marry women from the People of the Book, they may use this permission as an excuse to have relationships with them. Islam does indeed hold the People of the Book (Jews and Christians) in special regard and allows Muslim men to marry Jewish or Christian women, but this permission is not unconditional. Leaving aside any debate as to whether the Jews and Christians of today are like the Jews and Christians of the Prophet's time, and bearing in mind the Islamic teaching that fornication is forbidden, we should remind ourselves of the verse in the Qur'an that says:

﴿ٱلْيَوْمَ أُحِلَّ لَكُمُ ٱلطَّيِّبَٰتُ وَطَعَامُ ٱلَّذِينَ أُوتُوا۟ ٱلْكِتَٰبَ حِلٌّ لَّكُمْ وَطَعَامُكُمْ حِلٌّ لَّهُمْ وَٱلْمُحْصَنَٰتُ مِنَ ٱلْمُؤْمِنَٰتِ وَٱلْمُحْصَنَٰتُ مِنَ ٱلَّذِينَ أُوتُوا۟ ٱلْكِتَٰبَ مِن قَبْلِكُمْ إِذَآ ءَاتَيْتُمُوهُنَّ أُجُورَهُنَّ مُحْصِنِينَ غَيْرَ مُسَٰفِحِينَ وَلَا مُتَّخِذِىٓ أَخْدَانٍ وَمَن يَكْفُرْ بِٱلْإِيمَٰنِ فَقَدْ حَبِطَ عَمَلُهُ وَهُوَ فِى ٱلْءَاخِرَةِ مِنَ ٱلْخَٰسِرِينَ ﴿٥﴾ ﴾ (سورة المائدة: ٥)

❨This day are [all] things good and pure made lawful unto you. The food of the People of the Book is lawful unto you and yours is lawful unto them. [Lawful unto you in marriage] are [not only] chaste women who are believers, but chaste women among the People of the Book, revealed before your time — when you give them their due dowers, and desire chastity, not lewdness, nor secret intrigues. If anyone rejects faith, fruitless is his work, and in the Hereafter he will be in the ranks of those who have lost [all spiritual good].❩   *(Qur'an 5: 5)*

The specification is that if a Muslim bride is not chosen, only chaste Jewish or Christian women are acceptable partners for marriage. The Qur'an spells out the conditions for such marriages quite clearly: ❨when you give them their due dowers, and desire chastity, not lewdness, nor secret intrigues❩. There is no room whatsoever for 'having a good time' or 'sowing one's wild oats'.

Dowries: Don't price yourself out of the market!

Interestingly, one of the scholars I consulted about this matter said that describing non-Muslim women as "easy" could be taken to refer to the fact that they are unlikely to demand exorbitant dowries, sets of jewellery, and so forth, and in that sense they are "easier" to marry.[2] The dowry issue is known to be a major barrier to marriage in many Muslim countries, as many girls' families demand ever-increasing amounts of wealth. Girls have "priced themselves out of the market", and men find it hard to find a wife due to all the subsequent hassles and difficulties that it involves. It is suggested that the fact that non-Muslim women are "easier" to marry in this sense is in fact within "the spirit of Islam, which seeks to make it easy for young people to get married and raise a family".[3] Action clearly needs to be taken to put an end to excessive dowry demands, so that it will be easier for Muslim men to find Muslim spouses.

What about the children?

However, the idea that Muslim men may find Western non-Muslim women "easier to marry" raises many other issues: what about the Muslim women who are left behind because of family/

cultural issues? And what about the children; is there any guarantee that they will have a solid Islamic upbringing? Although many Western women who marry Muslim men do embrace Islam or at least agree to raise the children as Muslims, there are also cases where the women have sought to 'Christianise' the children with the matter ending in court, accusations flying, all concerned being deeply hurt, and fathers and children being separated.[4]

"Impure women are for impure men..."

The fact that many who come to the West, 'sow their wild oats' and then expect to find a young virgin from back home to marry is a reflection of individual arrogance and ignorance of Islam. The Qur'an (24: 3) states that a man who is guilty of fornication or adultery should not marry anybody except a woman who is similarly guilty; Allah (ﷻ) also says:

﴿ٱلْخَبِيثَتُ لِلْخَبِيثِينَ وَٱلْخَبِيثُونَ لِلْخَبِيثَتِ وَٱلطَّيِّبَتُ لِلطَّيِّبِينَ وَٱلطَّيِّبُونَ لِلطَّيِّبَتِ ... ﴾

(سورة النُّور: ٢٦)

﴿Impure women are for impure men, and impure men for impure women, and women of purity are for men of purity, and men of purity are for women of purity...﴾   *(Qur'an 24: 26)*

In modern terms, anyone who has 'a past' does not deserve to demand a 'pure' bride. This should be borne in mind by all those who seek to arrange marriages. We should also think in terms of educating our young people before they get to the age when they might be tempted to behave in a reckless fashion. After all, as the English saying goes, it is no use shutting the stable door after the horse has bolted!

Those who live in glass houses should not throw stones...

Another issue that is seldom raised is one that often goes hand-in-hand with the "let's-rip-off-the-unbelievers" approach: namely, the revoltingly smug and self-righteous attitude adopted by some Muslims who love to look down their noses at the West and condemn the moral laxity they see there, whilst assuming that such things never happen in Muslim societies. The sad fact is that they do, although perhaps to a lesser extent than in Western societies.

What are we doing about it?

Just a brief glance at the historical and cultural factors contributing to an amoral if not immoral social environment makes it clear that many Westerners have had little or no moral grounding, and it is no wonder. Many churches offer little or minimal — or worse — inconsistent moral leadership; many public schools can be no better, with secularised curricula, declining resources, embattled, disillusioned teachers and escalating drug and crime problems; and as for politicians and royalty, in many cases, they are the ones who provide the raw material for the stories that sell sleazy newspapers! Who is going to show the people of the West a better way? Have we Muslims done anything about it? Have we shown them a true picture of Islam and what it has to offer in the way of solutions to the social problems they face? We should realise that Muslims are not immune from these same problems (including drugs, alcoholism, and so on), especially if we live in the West and neglect our children's tarbiyah! We may have talked about reaching out, but are we really doing anything about it?

It has been several decades since Mawdudi told us that "the need to witness God's guidance before mankind remains as necessary and as urgent as ever."[5] Things certainly have not improved in all this time! Our duty is to be witnesses before humanity, both in word and deed. We talk an awful lot, but actions speak louder than words. We are clearly neglecting our duties. Far from hurling accusations and taking advantage of Westerners, who themselves are often victims of their societies' ills, we are supposed to be leading the way!

﴿كُنتُمْ خَيْرَ أُمَّةٍ أُخْرِجَتْ لِلنَّاسِ تَأْمُرُونَ بِالْمَعْرُوفِ وَتَنْهَوْنَ عَنِ الْمُنكَرِ

... ﴿١١٠﴾﴾   (سورة آل عِمرَان : ١١٠)

﴿You are the best of peoples, evolved for humankind, enjoining what is right, forbidding what is wrong...﴾   *(Qur'an 3: 110)*

Time to review our attitudes

The widespread attitude that it is acceptable for Muslims to abuse and cheat non-Muslims because they are "just unbelievers after all" also needs to be addressed. Not only that, but years of being sold rancid meat and shrivelled vegetables has shown me that there are Muslims in business who see nothing wrong with short-changing fellow-Muslims who happen to be of a different ethnic origin or speak a different language. This is an appalling state of affairs! What kind of picture of Islam are we presenting with our actions that speak louder than words?

In fact, as long as non-Muslims are not hostile towards us, nor seeking to persecute us, destroy us or drive us out from our homes, we are obliged to treat them decently and fairly. In fact, the word used in the Qur'an, *tabarroohum*, which Yusuf 'Ali translates as ❨dealing kindly and justly with them❩ (see Qur'an 60: 8), is one of those Arabic terms that is difficult to translate with any one English word. As Yusuf Qaradawi explains, "it signifies that kindness and generosity which is over and above justice."[6] This would certainly rule out cheating and abusing non-Muslims.

Treachery

Such abuse may even be regarded as an act of betrayal. As Dr. Darsh points out, "Muslims living in non-Muslim lands are not allowed to cheat." He quotes the scholar Ibn Qudâmah as stating clearly that when a Muslim enters a non-Muslim land with a guarantee of security (which in modern terms may be taken to mean as visa), that security does not give him the freedom to cheat and abuse the people.[7]

Summary

There is no Islamic sanction whatsoever for abusing non-Muslims by cheating in business transactions or by 'using' non-Muslim women. Muslims should be honest and straightforward in their dealings with all people, whether they are Muslims or not. This is a message that is, to a large extent, ignored; it is one we must remind ourselves of and warn one another about. For a start, messages from the *minbar*[8] on Fridays would not go amiss.

CHAPTER SEVEN

Purdah to the Max: Home as Prison?

*M*any of the stereotypes surrounding Islam and Muslims focus on the idea of 'purdah'. This conjures up images of women swathed in robes and veils, hidden in the innermost recesses of homes and sultans' palaces, kept away from the gaze of strange men and the world outside. Such a life has certainly been the lot of some Muslim women in the past (and even in the present day), but does such a lifestyle have Islamic sanction?

'Purdah' is derived from a Persian and Urdu word *pardah*, which means curtain, veil or partition; hence its meaning is similar to that of the Arabic word 'hijab'. However, purdah is more often used to refer to the seclusion of women, as much as to the way they dress. (Such women are completely covered by a burka, on the very rare occasions when they do venture forth.) Interestingly, the word is defined in English as referring to the "Indian system of secluding women of rank from public view", as it entered the language when the British occupied India and found this system in place among Muslims and some Hindus who had adopted the practice. In fact, India is not the only Muslim or Muslim-influenced country where public space is viewed as belonging only to men. I have heard plenty of travellers' tales to the same effect about Pakistan, Afghanistan and Saudi Arabia, for example.

Hijab

The issue of dress is often included in any discussion on purdah, or more generally on women's roles and status. However, in this chapter I want to focus on the practice of purdah in the sense of seclusion. The issue of dress has been covered (no pun intended) elsewhere;[1] it is clear that women should dress modestly, covering everything except the face and hands whenever they go out or are in the presence of non-maḥram men. This is the minimum extent of what is meant by 'hijab'; some writers and scholars suggest that women must wear an outergarment (in the form of a jilbâb,[2] an abaya or a burka) when they go outside, and/or that they should cover their faces and hands as well.[3] Given the difficulties of wearing a hijab in the West (for example, sisters may be sworn at and abused in the street, or even denied education, employment or promotion), one may wonder about the wisdom of pressuring sisters to adopt the forms of veiling or covering that are seen by Westerners as more 'extreme' or 'exotic'. What we can say with certainty is that the 'basic hijab' (covering everything except the face and hands with loose and opaque garments) is essential and should be encouraged, whatever the specific style adopted. Local forms of veiling or covering are beginning to emerge among Muslims in the West, just as regional styles have evolved throughout the Muslim world.

A woman's place is...?

Moving on from how women should dress, we come to ideas about how they should behave and what their role and sphere should be. Muslims have a reputation for secluding their women, and although the motive may originally have been protection, the custom became (and in some areas/communities remains) stifling.

When one reads accounts of life in Madinah at the time of the Prophet (ﷺ), one has the distinct opinion that interaction between the sexes, whilst within Islamic bounds, was somewhat more relaxed than either the cultural norms that subsequently prevailed, or the 'ideal' society now advocated by many Islamic activists. The women of Madinah interacted — within Islamic limits, of course — with the men; they were free to attend the mosque, even for fajr and 'ishâ' prayers, to take part in battles (within certain constraints), and to speak up and ask the Prophet (ﷺ) about any and every aspect of life when they needed knowledge.

Contrast this picture with the current state of affairs, where the emphasis among many Muslims is on women staying in the home. There are mosques in which women are not allowed, and no provision is made for them whatsoever. There are entire communities where the women never attend Eid prayers, even though their attendance has been commanded by the Prophet (ﷺ), to the extent that according to the hadith narrated by Umm 'Atiyah, even menstruating women were encouraged to attend the gathering and share the joy of the occasion.[4] There are families where girls are not allowed to go to school for fear of their meeting boys, so knowledge is denied to them and the talents and potential given to them by Allah go to waste. There are Muslim communities — in the West! — where a woman cannot even go to the local store for some essential goods, for fear that tongues will wag and thus cause trouble between her and her husband. There are women rendered virtually helpless because their families, husbands and communities have 'infantilised' them in the name of religion.

How did we get into this mess?

What went wrong? Islam brought revolutionary changes: women were at last given dignity, respect, rights and a positive role; the worst excesses against them were curtailed; and justice in all matters, including polygyny and divorce, was decreed. How did we sink into this abyss? It has been suggested that the reasons may lie in the remarkable, rapid expanse of the frontiers of Islam during the first decades after the Prophet's death. The first Muslims were a tribal people, with the strong ties of kinship characteristic of tribal societies, and there was a sense of security that came from being among relatives and friends.[5] As Islam expanded and the Muslims moved into new lands, where urban civilisation had long held sway, these tribal people may have felt that things were going out of control. Living among strangers with different customs, one way to regain a sense of control might be to impose tighter restrictions on one's family members; this may well have been coupled with a genuine concern for the well-being and safety of the womenfolk in turbulent times (society "instinctively began protecting its women with great care").[6]

Furthermore, the lands to which Islam first spread had a long history of misogynistic attitudes, to some extent rooted in the Judeo-Christian tradition. For example, the customs of face-veiling and confining women to a 'harem' were adopted as status symbols. A man who could afford to keep his wife or wives secluded was obviously so rich that he did not need to rely on any economic contribution they could make. Families of the lower classes, however, depended not only on what the man could earn, but also on whatever the woman could grow or make, either for their own use or for sale. A family's very survival depended on the efforts of both husband and wife. Such families (the majority) could not afford to seclude their women and do without their contribution. When a family could afford not to have its womenfolk working, the women could be secluded as a status symbol — a sign of the family's wealth. Thus purdah could have spread as the lower classes emulated the practices of the elite.

Deep-rooted bias and moral conservatism

One scholar of history[7] has suggested that there was/is a deep-rooted bias against women in the lands where Islam first spread, and that this fuelled the reaction against the reforms brought by Islam. The reactionary attitudes that grew up may have been further exacerbated by the turmoil of the Mongol and Tatar invasions, when much of the Muslim world was laid to waste. In addition, in times of upheaval, moral conservatism may increase; indeed, when the world seems to be going out of control, it is perhaps understandable that men may try to regain a sense of control by imposing their will on the only people they can, that is, within the domestic sphere. Incidentally, this may explain why many immigrant parents are so strict with their children: they may feel overwhelmed by the strange new culture of the land they have moved to. As they may not understand the new society, they may fear it and feel out of control; whence the desire to at least gain or maintain control over the immediate family.[8]

If it is indeed the case that long-standing misogynistic tendencies resurfaced and took hold again so quickly, then perhaps, apart from the golden era of the time of the Prophet (ﷺ) and the Rightly-guided Caliphs, the true Islamic system has not yet prevailed. (One may compare this to the observation that Islamic egalitarianism has not taken firm root in the subcontinental Muslim cultures, as the caste system is alive and well among Muslims from those cultures).[9]

Perhaps the major root of the purdah issue is the way women are viewed: their entire bodies and even their voices are deemed to represent an overwhelming temptation and moral danger to men, so we must cover up and shut up (and put up with it)! In most traditional societies, and even to some extent in the West, the entire responsibility for protecting morality is placed squarely on our (supposedly delicate and weak) shoulders. That is astounding — are men so feeble-minded and weak-willed that they are so easily led astray? Placing the entire burden of upholding morality on women's shoulders is an idea that has crept into Islamic thought from Judeo-Christian sources, where Eve was held to be the cause of Adam's 'fall from grace' and every woman was considered, as a daughter of Eve, to be evil and the cause (actual or potential) of men's downfall.

Qur'anic priorities

Moreover, such notions of women's moral burden are in stark contrast to the Qur'an, where the command to lower one's gaze and guard one's modesty is given to men first. It is a scientific fact that men are more easily affected by visual stimuli, which is why the extent of women's *'awrah* (the part of a person's body that must be screened from public view) is greater than men's, but the fact remains that men are also supposed to behave and dress modestly, and in fact the command to do so comes to them before it is given to women.

وَقُل لِّلْمُؤْمِنِينَ يَغُضُّوا۟ مِنْ أَبْصَٰرِهِمْ وَيَحْفَظُوا۟ فُرُوجَهُمْ ذَٰلِكَ أَزْكَىٰ لَهُمْ إِنَّ ٱللَّهَ خَبِيرٌۢ بِمَا يَصْنَعُونَ ۝ وَقُل لِّلْمُؤْمِنَٰتِ يَغْضُضْنَ مِنْ أَبْصَٰرِهِنَّ وَيَحْفَظْنَ فُرُوجَهُنَّ وَلَا يُبْدِينَ زِينَتَهُنَّ إِلَّا مَا ظَهَرَ مِنْهَا ... ۝

(سورة النور: ٣٠-٣١)

❝Say to the believing men that they should lower their gaze and guard their modesty; that will make for greater purity for them; and Allah is well-acquainted with all that they do. And say to the believing women that they should lower their gaze and guard their modesty; that they should not display their beauty and ornaments except what [must ordinarily] appear thereof...❞ *(Qur'an 24: 30-31)*

Even one of the most 'hard-line' Muslim writers[10] I have come across points out that the injunction to lower the gaze is addressed to men first, and suggests that the majority of Muslim men do not obey this command, when he asks, "... can someone say with confidence that Muslim men lower their gaze upon seeing strange women?"[11]

Covered women have long had to endure inappropriate and discomforting stares from Muslim men, even in mosques and Islamic establishments (these are often hostile "what-are-you-doing-here?" glares as much as anything else). Sad to say, some Muslim countries have earned an unpleasant reputation for being places where even totally veiled women may be subjected to stares and touching. Whether a woman is covered or not, men have a responsibility to control themselves and lower their gaze. Blaming the woman is blatantly unfair. In most cases it would be apt to question whether we Muslims have fulfilled our duty of educating people, calling them to Islam and explaining to them why modesty is a good idea. If we have failed to convey the message with which we have been entrusted, how can we dare to blame those who do not have this knowledge?

Purdah = prison?

Whatever the style of hijab adopted, should a Muslim woman stay at home and never venture forth, as suggested by many and as actually practised in many cultures? If a woman lives in a fairly large house and has a supportive extended family around, then such a 'restricted' life may be bearable, although it still reeks of imprisonment, not to mention elitism; can only the wealthy attain such an ideal practice? For the rest of us, living in small apartments, often far away from family and friends, possibly with small children, no means of transport, and a husband whose job or study takes him away from the home for most of the day, such purdah would be nothing more than the cruelest of jail sentences. As the twentieth-century scholar Muhammad al-Ghazali pointed out in his well-known biography of the Prophet (ﷺ), confining women to their homes was the provisional punishment for illegal sexual activity *(Qur'an 4: 15)*, and so could not reasonably be asserted to be a standing order for all women. The women of Madinah certainly went out of their homes to work, to attend the mosque, to seek knowledge, and even to take part in jihad. Purdah in the sense of seclusion is, again, a class thing: rich families could/can afford to keep their women idle at home, whilst poorer families have always needed either the fruits of women's labour in the fields or the income from her work in order to survive.

Whilst the home is not meant to be a prison, it is definitely recommended that women's lives be home-based; that is, there should be no unnecessary or aimless hanging about in streets and malls, but going out to study, to work and for essential errands is acceptable. The 'hard-line' writer referred to above describes Maryam Jameelah, an American convert to Islam who emigrated to Pakistan in 1962, as wearing the burka, which covers everything including the face. Although a firm believer in segregation and a home-based life, Maryam Jameelah would go out to the local bazaar when necessary, and would also visit friends in the neighbourhood. She suggests that:

Purdah has been for many centuries in India and Pakistan interpreted too strictly and rigidly by traditional orthodox families — far beyond the actual requirements of the Shari'ah.[12]

Conditions for going out

If women are allowed to go out, what are the conditions? First of all, she should dress and behave properly, that is, she should wear a hijab (see above) and conduct herself in a decent manner. The purpose of her going out should be serious; for example, she should not hang about aimlessly in streets and malls; however, this applies equally to men, as all Muslims should be purposeful people who avoid wasting time in idle pursuits. Going to school and work are acceptable as long as one conducts oneself appropriately.

Many Muslims express concern about mixed schools, for example. Of course, single-sex institutions are preferable, but these are few and far between in the West, and numbers are declining. There are also alternatives: Islamic schools and institutions, home schooling, correspondence courses, and sending youngsters to school in Muslim countries are all options, none of which are perfect and foolproof, but all of which may be practical and preferable. A more radical suggestion, which I have heard from a number of parents, is to arrange early marriages (contrary to current practice) and let the newly-weds study together. There will be a permissible outlet for their 'youthful urges' and they will be able to encourage and support one another through their studies. The young wife, however, should not be over-burdened with domestic chores; if both partners are studying or working, then both partners should share the responsibility of keeping house. However, if all else fails, then the experience of many devout Muslim students in the West demonstrates that it is possible to attend co-ed schools and universities and have minimal contact with non-maḥram men. All one has to do is to have a solid grounding in Islamic etiquette (parents and educators, take note!) and to be firm about one's limits. There is much awareness about sexual harassment nowadays, which has led to women and girls becoming more assertive of their right to resist and challenge unwanted touching, and even speech or jokes that make them feel uncomfortable. Most institutions have guidelines about harassment and will take action against those who transgress, so Muslims would do well to be familiar with the procedures in their school or workplace.

Wherever possible: single-sex institutions

Single sex institutions and service provision are preferable for Muslim women and men, and indeed, many non-Muslims would prefer them too. The British newspaper *Daily Mail* has long campaigned against mixed wards in hospitals; when its campaign began in the 1990s it found itself leading a groundswell of opinion. Many people came forward with tales of harrowing experiences in mixed wards and added their voices to the campaign. In May 2008, the *Daily Mail* reported that eleven years after the government pledged to end mixed wards, two-thirds of British hospitals were still failing to offer proper single-sex accommodation to patients.[13]

In the field of education, many are increasingly aware of the fact that girls do better when there are no boys around, especially in subjects such as mathematics. There have been many studies showing that both boys and girls do better in single-sex classrooms than in a co-ed setting. The US-based National Association for Single Sex Public Education has a wealth of information on its website (www.singlesexschools.org), quoting a number of studies in the US, Britain and Australia that demonstrate the advantages of single-sex schooling for both girls and boys. Where there is no other option, it is still possible to maintain minimal contact with the opposite sex in such institutions, as suggested above; parents need to educate their children — sons as well as daughters — as to what is acceptable behaviour.

Instilling an awareness of Allah and nurturing the child's own spirituality and Islamic identity will be far more effective than merely imposing dictates. Given the fact that most human societies (not just the Muslim ones) implicitly expect girls to be somewhat meek and submissive, we should also give some thought to empowering girls to be able to stand up for their beliefs.

Women and work

Whilst a home-based life may be preferable for some Muslim women, there are always women who need to work. This may be for economic reasons: in the West, the prevalent belief is that most families need two incomes to maintain a decent standard of living, although there is now some movement in Western society away from this idea (downsizing is not just a corporate issue!), for example, books such as *The Heart Has Its Own Reasons*[14] and *Staying Home Instead*[15] have appeared as a reaction against the pontifications of 'childless career feminists' who called for women to have and do it all without any real knowledge of the lives of the majority of women who still have husbands and babies. In traditional societies, women's labour in the fields has often been essential for the family's very survival. Home-based work, or even setting up one's own home-based business, may be a good idea for Muslim women, especially those with young children.

An often overlooked fact is that many women feel the need to work for their own personal fulfilment; there are those among us who would go crazy at home, — boredom, isolation, the lack of intelligent adult conversation and the absence of intellectual stimulation! Home-based work is one solution, but as we are always hearing of the need for Muslim women doctors, nurses, teachers, social workers, counsellors, and so on, there is a need for some Muslim women to work outside the home. Some of these women will also be mothers, so there is also a need for Muslim child-care facilities, which is an ideal 'business' to run from home.

The advent of Internet has been a blessing for millions of women who do prefer to stay at home, but who like to keep active through involvement in online Islamic networks and support groups, participating in distance learning courses, or even working at jobs that involve telecommuting. Nevertheless, staying at home cannot be a universal rule when we need women to fulfil important functions outside the home; some women will have to go out of their homes to get the education and training they need, and then to work in these important areas.

The emphasis on the role of the stay-at-home mother also marginalizes those sisters who cannot have children and adds to the pain they are already feeling. We must also promote other roles for women that any woman can fulfil. 'Â'ishah bint Abi Bakr (ﷺ), a major source of Islamic knowledge and hadiths, did not have children but was able to make a great contribution to

Islam. We should take care to validate all roles that are within Islamic limits.

Going out for *tabarruj* is forbidden

It has been pointed out that the restrictions and conditions that the Qur'an and the Sunnah have placed on women's going out are specifically for cases where the intention is to make a 'wanton display' of oneself (in Arabic, *tabarruj*).[16] Although later scholars have extended this to imply a blanket prohibition on all going out, it is clear from the example of the first Muslims that women did go out for legitimate reasons, such as seeking knowledge, working, and even for jihad, and they did so with the explicit permission and approval of the Prophet (ﷺ).

Free mixing is not permitted

Saying that women may go out, however, does NOT condone free mixing such as that which goes on in Western societies and even in certain communities of 'modern' Muslims. Islam takes the 'prevention is better than cure' approach. When it forbids an act, such as adultery or fornication, it also forbids its followers from doing things that may lead to the forbidden act. In this case, prohibitions on dressing and behaving provocatively, mixing freely, and being alone with a non-maḥram member of the opposite sex are practical measures imposed to prevent the greater evil. The appalling consequences of unrestrained free mixing need not be dwelt on here; no one can be unaware of the social devastation that it can cause, including broken homes, unwed mothers and so forth.

Mosque attendance

It is clear from the accounts of the time of the Prophet (ﷺ) that the entire community regularly gathered in the mosque; women were not excluded from community affairs. Limits were clearly laid down, however; when the Prophet (ﷺ) saw that men and women were mingling as they came out of the mosque, he told the women to keep to the edges of the road. Men were also prohibited from walking between two women, and the Prophet (ﷺ) and his Companions adopted the practice of remaining behind in the mosque to allow the women time to leave, to further prevent any chance of mingling.[17]

Men and women also sat separately in the mosque and at other gatherings. There are instances when the Prophet (ﷺ), having spoken to the people, felt that his words had not reached the women, so he would go over to where the women were and address them specifically.[18]

Jihad

Far from having to remain in their houses until the end of their lives, (which, as we have read, was a punishment for adultery and could not have been meant as a permanent situation for all women) the first Muslim women were also able to take part in jihad. There were conditions attached to their participation, but these were practical matters concerned with their safety: they were to be accompanied by members of their family or tribe (in one case the presence of other women was sufficient), and they had to have the express permission of the Prophet (ﷺ). In most cases their role was one of support — to cook, bring water to the thirsty fighters, tend the wounded, and so on. One Companion, Rufaydah

(☙), even established and ran the first military field hospital, where she and other women performed surgery and administered other emergency medical care.[19] Their services were to be confined to their own family members wherever possible. If an emergency arose and they had to deal with non-maḥram men, then it was to be within Islamic limits and, although medical emergencies constitute one of the exceptions to the usual rules, there was still to be the minimum of physical contact. Although women were not required or expected to bear arms or fight in the front line, they did so when they had to, and were commended by the Prophet (☙) for doing so. He spoke of Nusaybah bint Ka'b (☙), who fought fiercely to defend him during the battle of Uḥud; and at Ḥunayn, when he saw Umm Sulaym carrying a dagger and asked her why, he received the spirited reply, "If any unbeliever comes near me, I will rip open his belly!"[20] This may come as a surprise to many, but with the full blessing of the Prophet (he prophesied that it would happen), Umm Sulaym's sister, Umm Ḥarâm, even accompanied her husband 'Ubâdah ibn aṣ-Ṣâmit to Syria and Palestine, and participated in the first retaliatory attack by the fledgling Muslim navy against the Roman fleet in Cyprus — she was martyred there.[21]

Da'wah

Another issue that we should mention, although briefly, is *da'wah*.[22] It seems that many Muslims, in their enthusiasm to spread the word, will engage in lengthy conversations with people of the opposite sex. It is particularly infuriating to see men (whose wives may well be 'in purdah') chatting with young females in colleges and universities on the basis that they are "doing da'wah". Whatever our intentions, we must always remain within the limits of Islam; and whilst we may be reluctant to appear rude or seem to be brushing people off, it is better, once we are sure that the person's interest in Islam is genuine, to direct him/her to knowledgeable Muslims of their own sex. Whilst there is no bashfulness in matters pertaining to religious rulings, in today's crazy world it is better to err on the side of caution and have such information conveyed in a one-on-one or small group situation by people of the same sex. (This is the example of the Prophet [鐄] and his Companions; see Chapter 9.)

It is not too difficult, when a fellow-student or colleague of the opposite sex is asking questions about Islam, to offer to introduce them to other Muslim men or women, and if you can find converts who come from a similar background, this can be of immense help. Most genuine seekers after truth will appreciate this opportunity.

Summary

'Total purdah' — keeping women shut up in the house and denying them the opportunity to fulfil their potential and make a contribution to society — is not even Islamic. Women have a lot more to offer than producing babies and cooking fancy meals. Our skills, intellect, insight, and so forth, are vital to the well-being of the community and of the Ummah. Islam recognises the complementary roles of the male and female. Why should we shut off 50% of our human resources? Men and women are allowed to have contact when necessary for the purposes of education, work, and furthering the Islamic cause.[23] Hijab and the clearly laid-out restrictions define the limits within which we can work; these restrictions, in fact, are meant to and often prove to be liberating, in that we are no longer objects on display, and we can just get on with the work at hand.

CHAPTER EIGHT

The Unkindest Cut:
Female Circumcision

*I*t was the early 80s, and I was a new Muslim, a very raw recruit indeed. Hijab still felt strange, and it was as if everyone was staring at me. It was a time of upheaval, a time when I was still acutely self-conscious and a little unsure of the 'new me'. One of several issues I had heard dark mutterings about was 'female circumcision' and Islam; I could not imagine how the two went together, and was not even sure what 'female circumcision' was. When a female anthropologist recently from East Africa put on an exhibition about female circumcision in the university, I thought this would be the prefect opportunity to find out what all the fuss was about.

On that particular occasion, I did not have the opportunity to learn very much. As I was peering at the photos and accompanying text, and finding it hard to believe what I was reading, I was accosted by the anthropologist herself, who demanded to know who I was and why I was dressed this way. When she realised that I was English and had willingly embraced Islam, she became extremely angry, virtually accused me of being insane, and wanted to know how I could possibly have embraced a religion that did such terrible things to its women!

Over the years, the feminist vitriol has abated somewhat, at least as far as Islam and female circumcision is concerned. Many activists and reporters now make it clear that female circumcision is not a specifically Muslim issue. There are also Muslim scholars who speak out against the practice, particularly the more extreme forms. What is more, in November 2006, the Shaykh 'Ali Gomaa, the Grand Mufti of Egypt, and Mohammad Sayed Tantawi, the Grand Shaykh of Al-Azhar in Egypt, each issued a fatwa stating that even the mildest form of female circumcision was not part of the Sunnah, and that excision and infibulation (defined below) were absolutely prohibited in Islam. Other scholars agreed, and explained that since the practice resulted in bodily and psychological harm, it would be considered forbidden according to Islamic law. Several months later, after a young girl died as a result of infection after undergoing genital cutting, the Grand Mufti issued a stronger fatwa in which he declared that it was completely forbidden.[1] However, some scholars caution that trying to implement a total ban on the practice in societies where it is deeply entrenched might result in simply 'driving the practice underground', which would make it even more difficult to combat and root out.[2] On the other side of this issue, some Western feminists and liberals are even beginning to question whether they really have the right to impose their white, middle-class values on women of other societies and cultures.

Female genital mutilation — Definitions

So, what is female circumcision or, as it is also and increasingly known, 'female genital mutilation (FGM)'? Several procedures, varying in severity, are in fact grouped together under this name. It is important to be aware of the distinctions:[3]

1. Circumcision (this is sometimes called 'Sunnah'): This involves removing the hood or tip of the clitoris. It is the mildest of the procedures known as 'female circumcision', and is the only form that may be regarded as having any kind of Islamic sanction, being mentioned in a weak hadith (see below) as a practice that the Prophet (ﷺ) allowed.

2. Excision: This is an 'intermediate' operation in which the clitoris and all or part of the labia minora are removed. This has no basis in Islam, is detrimental to the woman, and thus forbidden by Islamic law.[4]

3. Infibulation: This is the most radical procedure: the clitoris, labia minora, and at least the anterior two-thirds of the labia majora are removed. The two sides of what remains of the vulva are then pinned or sutured together, leaving a small (often inadequate) opening for the passage of urine and menstrual blood. Upon marriage, the infibulated woman has to be 'opened up' with a knife or other instrument.[5] She has to be 'opened up' to deliver a baby, and will be re-stitched after childbirth. This horrific procedure cannot be sanctioned by any Islamic text, and is definitely *harâm*.[6]

It is important to make a clear distinction between the first procedure described above and the more extreme operations. For the purpose of this discussion, I will use the word 'circumcision' to refer to the minimal operation which, according to some scholars, was allowed, but not enjoined or encouraged by the Prophet (ﷺ), and female genital mutilation or FGM to refer to the more extreme procedures.

Not unique to Muslim cultures

It is those two more extreme procedures that give rise to the most concern, and these are the ones that are usually focused on by critics when female circumcision is discussed. These are also the procedures for which there is no basis whatsoever in Islamic teaching, although Islam is often blamed for the practice. In fact, 'female circumcision' is practised by people of many religions — Christians and animists, as well as Muslims — in the regions where it is common, so it cannot be described as a uniquely 'Islamic' phenomenon. Female circumcision is common in several parts of Africa, notably Egypt, Sudan, Somalia and Ethiopia. It is also known in parts of Arabia and in Malaysia and Indonesia.[7] However, in other parts of the Muslim world, such as Syria and Pakistan, for example, it is unknown. The custom is one of great antiquity: it is mentioned by Herodotus (seventh century BCE)[8] and is regarded by many as dating back to Pharaonic times. Curiously enough, clitoridectomy (removal of the clitoris) was a common procedure until fairly recent times in the West, as a cure for 'hysteria' and other vaguely-defined ailments,[9] and there are strange reports from mediaeval times of the lengths knights would go to in order to guarantee the fidelity of their wives and daughters whilst they were away fighting battles (chastity belts and all that). Hence it should be clear that FGM is not a uniquely Islamic custom, although, regrettably, many Muslims believe FGM to be Islamically sanctioned.

A girl's ordeal

The trauma of such radical surgery is compounded by the fact that these operations are almost always carried out in non-sterile conditions, with old or rusty implements, by traditional 'midwives' who have little, if any, knowledge of proper surgical procedures. Anaesthesia is virtually unknown, and infection is an ever-present threat, in addition to the severe trauma caused by such radical surgery.

In most cultures where circumcision or FGM is practised, the operation usually takes place in early girlhood, before the onset of puberty (menarche). It is a leitmotif in the writings of modern Arab feminist writers, notably Nawal El Saadawi, who uses this and other women's issues as a stick with which to beat Islam, and is a favourite topic among anthropologists. Circumcision represents just one part of a whole socio-cultural belief system regarding relationships between the sexes, femininity, virginity, and so on. Some critics and activists would like to see the whole lot come tumbling down, of course. However, looking at these important issues, one can see that the popular beliefs among Muslim communities where these procedures are common may have their starting-point in Islamic values (such as the importance of chastity and segregation of the sexes, for example), although they may have been taken to extremes and/or distorted along the way by being mixed with local pre-Islamic or non-Islamic ideas and customs.

Medical and psychological consequences

When we turn to the medical and psychological consequences of FGM, we can see that these procedures cause more problems than they are supposed to solve.

Medical: As stated above, most procedures are carried out in unsanitary conditions. In the autumn of 1995, I watched a Canadian-made documentary on female circumcision on CBC-TV in which footage of an actual circumcision was shown, with the worst details blanked out (although viewers still had to endure hearing the child's screams). The operation was carried out in an earthen-floored hut in Ethiopia. Nawal El Saadawi, from a middle-class Egyptian family, describes her own circumcision taking place in the family's bathroom.[10] Anaesthesia is uncommon, although one writer describes a Sudanese midwife using proper surgical sutures, lint, and so forth, having received some medical training from the government. This midwife also told the anthropologist of methods used in the past: no anaesthesia and, in the case of infibulation, the use of thorns to hold the flesh together.[11] No doubt such unsanitary practices still prevail in some areas of the world.

Needless to say, infection is an ever-present threat. There is also the risk of error at the hands of untrained *dayas* (traditional midwives) leading to severe haemorrhaging and shock (in both the medical and psychological senses). Infertility, chronic pelvic infections and menstrual problems are also mentioned frequently.

Complications also arise, inevitably, when these excised and infibulated women marry and have children. One can barely imagine the trauma involved in getting married in the first place; suffice it to say that one writer refers to a special "honeymoon hut" far enough removed from other dwellings that no one will be able to hear the bride's screams.[12]

Western doctors who have to treat infibulated women may find the experience shocking. Dr. Mary McCaffery, a London obstetrician, wondered how a baby could "get out of a tiny hole surrounded by scar tissue".[13] This doctor operates to remove scar tissue several weeks before the baby is due. The operation takes place under general anaesthetic, but even then, "some of the women scream when their genitals are touched. The pain is not just physical — it goes very, very deep and will be with them forever."[14]

Moral/psychological: The comment quoted above also indicates that the trauma experienced by circumcised/infibulated women goes beyond the physical. Sexual frigidity is not uncommon; so it is clear that although this practice is supposed to guarantee the virginity of brides, it is hardly conducive to a satisfying married life — a right that Islam gives to both men and women.

The Islamic perspective:
Female circumcision in the hadiths

Turning towards the Islamic perspective on this issue, there are no hadiths in either Bukhari or Muslim that instruct the circumcision of women.[15] Circumcision is mentioned, indirectly, in Bukhari. In the Book of Bathing (*ghusl*), there is a hadith that contains the wording, *idhâ iltaqâ al-khitânân* "When the two circumcised parts meet", referring to the necessity of *ghusl* — a ritual shower — following sexual relations, even if there is no ejaculation.[16] There is a hadith narrated by Muslim with this wording that has been cited by some as indicative that the practice was known in early Islamic times, and that since the Prophet (ﷺ) mentioned it, it meant that he approved of it. However, the scholars of Islam are also scholars of the Arabic language, and one of them gave this explanation for the term (*al-khitânân*, the two circumcised parts) used in the hadith:

> This authentic hadith is by no means evidence of legitimacy, the Arabic word used for "the two circumcision organs" is in the dual case and it follows the habit of calling two objects or two persons after the more familiar or after either of them, giving it prominence. There are many examples of this in

idiomatic Arabic usage, such as "the two Umars", referring to Abu Bakr and Umar; "the two moons", referring to the sun and moon; "the shining two", making the same reference although the moon does not shine of itself and only reflects the light of the sun; "the two 'ishas", referring to maghreb and 'isha, and "the two zhuhrs", referring to zhuhr and 'asr. Arabs usually choose the more prominent of the two or the easier in giving a dual form, and that is why they say for parents, "the two fathers", although they are a father and a mother. Sometimes they choose the easier to pronounce as in their saying, "the two Umars" or the greater in status, such as in God's saying, "Nor are the two seas alike, the one being potable and pleasant to drink, and the other salty and briny". The first of these "two seas" is a river and the second, an actual sea. Sometimes the word with the female gender is chosen to make the dual form, such as in the expression "the two Marwas", referring to the two hills of As-Safa and Al-Marwa in Mecca. This usage in the Arabic language is familiar to Arabic linguists.[17]

According to this explanation, then, the hadith cannot be used in support of the practice of female circumcision in any form. It is worth remembering that, whilst the practice was not unheard of in Arabia, none of the women of the Prophet's (ﷺ) household was circumcised.[18]

The only hadith that directly mentions "female circumcision" is one that scholars have said is unreliable; it refers to a woman of Madinah who was known to perform the mildest procedure, which advocates of female genital cutting later began calling "Sunnah". The Prophet (ﷺ) told her: "Just touch, do not obliterate. This is more liked by the husband, and more radiant to the face."[19] Whatever the case, it does indicate that if the practice is to be followed at all — and the majority of scholars do not regard it as an obligation — then the minimal, least invasive procedure is to be followed. It may almost be viewed as a token gesture.

Excision and infibulation, which constitute an act of extreme mutilation, endanger the life of the child, and leave her with a lifelong legacy of pain and stress, are definitely not a part of the Islamic framework for women. Scholars from the classical period of Islamic jurisprudence like Ibn Ḥâzm and Ibn Qudâmah made it clear that cutting off or damaging a girl's or woman's labia is a crime that requires the payment of blood money or even retaliation in kind (!), which puts it in the category of the most heinous crimes, along with murder, mutilation, and rape.[20] Islam liberated women from the bondage of pre-Islamic ignorance and gave them the right to life, worship and education. How, then could anyone dare to imagine that such a horrific assault on their very femininity would have religious sanction!

Only the scholars can state for sure whether this minimal procedure (which, according to the hadith referred to above, may not even constitute clitoridectomy as such, as it does not remove the whole clitoris) should be allowed or not — and I am not a scholar. The "just touch" hadith is doubtful, according to scholars, and because in too many cases the procedure goes far beyond the 'Sunnah', there is also some debate as to whether the permissibility of even the mildest form of female circumcision should be suspended.[21] What we can be sure about is that female circumcision is **not** a Sunnah.

It is a sad fact that in many cultures where infibulation is practised, the commonly-held but mistaken view is that it is commanded by the Qur'an (as opposed to hadiths); the interviewer in the CBC documentary referred to above was shown stopping Somali immigrants in the foyer of a Toronto apartment building and quizzing them about this custom; virtually all of those who responded replied that it was a religious requirement laid down by the Qur'an. However, it must be borne in mind that this practice is most widespread in regions where illiteracy is not uncommon, and a greater percentage of women than men are unable to read (it seems that when times are tough, girls' education is always one of the first things to be jettisoned). If people are illiterate in their own language, they are unlikely to be able to read and understand the Arabic of the Qur'an, either. As it is the women who perpetrate and perpetuate the custom of female circumcision, and it is women who are most likely in traditional cultures to be uneducated, there are obviously major obstacles in the way of correcting this widely held misconception.

Are all women temptresses?

The messages given by a society that subjects its women to FGM appear particularly appalling: that a woman is a "weak, morally inferior being, oversexed and inherently inclined to wantonness, devoted to sensuality."[22] Similar sentiments are to be found in traditional Christian thought, where Eve (and, by extension, all women) is still blamed for the downfall of Adam (and, by extension, all men). It is obvious, to some of us at least, that just as some women are guilty of wantonness, so the men who participate in illicit acts with them must also be guilty; it is monstrously unfair to condemn all women (half of the human race!) for the misdeeds of a few of their number. Islam in its purest form, that is, at the time of the Prophet (ﷺ), treated men and women as equal, although different; men and women alike were, and are, told to preserve their chastity.

Islamic ideals versus social reality

Although Islam demands chastity from both men and women, and views both men and women as having sexual desire, societies that practice FGM place undue emphasis on female virginity. As in most societies, a double standard is at work so that, to a greater or lesser extent, the burden of maintaining chastity and the family 'honour' rests on women, whilst men are free to do as they please. Most of the reasons given for continuing this custom of FGM revolve around these issues of female virginity and family honour. The traditional view is that FGM or lesser forms of genital cutting will reduce the female libido, which otherwise would be rampantly out of control, threatening social stability. Far from curbing interest in such matters, however, some writers suggest that this kind of ignorance and suppression will actually exaggerate the role of sex so that women in these cultures may become abnormally obsessed with the matter, whereas others with a more balanced and normal upbringing and outlook will view sex as just one part of life.[23]

The Islamic view is certainly that the sexual urge is a normal part of the human condition, male and female, and one that is to be controlled and channelled via marriage. Islam similarly imposes limits or checks on food, drink, wealth and even worship — monkish asceticism is not part of the Islamic tradition.

Maintaining chastity in society:
The Islamic solution

Clearly there are those who fear the consequences of leaving women uncircumcised, but there is an answer to those concerns: the key is EDUCATION. Girls and women must be educated in true Islamic morals and values; needless to say, men and boys need this knowledge too. There is no place in Islam for the double standard, regardless of how prevalent this is today in both East and West. But this education must go beyond religious and moral teachings. There is a saying in English, "The devil finds work for idle hands." It applies to minds and bodies too. Girls (and boys) who are denied a decent education and never have an opportunity to fulfil their potential will naturally look for other diversions, of which pursuit of the opposite sex may well be one.

We, as parents, teachers and elders, must see to it that our children receive a sound education and are provided with ways of profitably using their leisure time. Watching the latest offerings from Hollywood (or Bollywood) does not count! Arts and crafts, sports, reading and voluntary work are all pastimes that can be encouraged in order to divert excess energy that might otherwise find its outlets in unacceptable channels. There is also the method suggested by the Prophet (ﷺ) to a young man who could not afford to marry yet feared that his youthful urges may lead him astray: fasting. Worship should not be the preserve only of the old who sense the approach of death and want to make up for lost time. How much better if good habits are instilled in all of us from an early age. Life is too short!

Speaking out

As the debate rumbles on, scholars have spoken out louder and more firmly against FGM. As I mentioned, eminent scholars at the highly-regarded Al-Azhar University have described the practice of FGM as "ḥarâm and un-Islamic".[24] In the West, Muslim community leaders are also taking a stance against such customs. In Toronto, home to large Somali and Ethiopian Muslim communities, Abdullah Hakim Quick has frequently spoken out, and has made the salient point that, although preservation of honour is often cited as the motive for continuing to 'circumcise' girls, decency comes from Islam, not from cultural practice.[25]

In the meantime, we can be sure that the extreme forms of female circumcision, excision and infibulation, are forbidden and criminal acts. They are described in Egypt and nearby countries as "Pharaonic" after all, and was not Pharaoh the enemy, the antithesis, of Islam?

Eradication: the way forward?

But what is the answer in societies where these customs are practised? Some feminists are beginning to question what right they have to dictate their liberal Western values to cultures which are so different to their own,[26] and in Holland, some liberals want to allow immigrants to continue practising FGM because banning their customs would be "racist".[27] When the uncircumcised girl risks being ostracised by her society and remaining unmarried, maybe retaining the minimal procedure would be preferable; but it bears repeating that this procedure is not commanded or even encouraged by Islam.

There is no doubt that the appalling abuse of excision and infibulation should be eradicated. Sound Islamic education (not Western feminism) can achieve this. It is encouraging to learn that migrant workers who have spent time in Saudi Arabia and been exposed to more orthodox interpretations of Islam return home and speak out against such mutilation carried out in the name of religion.[28] But given that female circumcision is part of marriage and gender roles, and that beliefs concerning its importance are very deeply-rooted, it is unlikely to be eradicated overnight. There are examples in Islamic history of a gradual approach to wiping out undesirable but widespread practices (for example, the gradual banning of alcohol). Again, education is required. Both men and women must be taught self-control; then there will be less need for artificial means to be imposed and enforced from without.

Muslim immigrants in the West: "children at risk?"

Another area of concern involves immigrant communities in the West who seek to continue this custom in their new homeland. The laws of most Western countries allow the authorities to remove a child who is regarded as being 'at risk' from the family home, and place him/her in a foster home. Both "Sunnah" and FGM are likely to be regarded by Westerners as a form of child abuse, and there is the possibility of children being removed from their family homes. In such circumstances, there is no guarantee that a child will be placed with Muslim foster-parents. Many social services providers (especially in Britain) categorise people on the basis of race, which could result, for example, in a 'black' Somali Muslim child being placed with 'black' Jamaican Christian foster parents. This is beginning to change: authorities are increasingly aware of the importance of Islam to Muslims. But parents from backgrounds where female circumcision is a part of the culture need, perhaps, to be made aware of this possibility. Which is worse, discarding an un-Islamic practice or running the risk of losing your child altogether?

Summary

In conclusion, we can say that female circumcision is not a requirement of Islam the way that male circumcision is. Although it is mentioned in one hadith, it is not a practice that is encouraged. In societies where it is a major part of the culture, simply eradicating it is not enough because FGM does not exist in isolation; it is part of a network of beliefs and practices surrounding virginity, marriage and 'honour'. The societies concerned require positive education that is rooted firmly in Islam. This is a need that must be addressed.

CHAPTER NINE

Beyond Home Economics:
Education for Girls and Women

$\mathcal{S}$he was another Muslim mother, somewhat shy, but over the weeks our tentative smiles and salams in the school yard grew into friendly chats as we waited for our children. From her traditional demeanour and slightly accented English, I assumed at first that she had come to this country as a bride, and had learned English since. In fact, I admired her for her proficiency in the language.

As I got to know her better, I found that I had to revise my assumptions (which in itself taught me a lesson). I found out that her family had immigrated when she was an infant. Then one day the bombshell dropped. She joined me as I was looking at the PTA notice-board, and when I made a comment about one of the posters she told me, "I do not know how to read!" I was astounded, but I had heard of children falling through the educational net and ending up as non-readers even though they had attended school. It happened to children of all backgrounds, for many reasons. I asked her whether extended visits back home (not uncommon among immigrants from South Asia) had caused her to miss a lot of her schooling. No, came the reply; she had not missed school because her parents had never sent her to school in the first place!

Feeling an increasing sense of despair for her, I tried to find out if there was anything to redeem this appalling situation. Home-schooling had never been an option. Although her brothers had been sent to school, the dreadful truth was that her parents, themselves uneducated, had simply seen no need to give their daughter even the most basic education. This situation had escaped the attention of education officers, who presumably were unaware of her very existence, and from a very early age, all my friend had done was cook and keep house. Whilst I had grown up surrounded by books in a family where literacy was taken for granted, my sister in faith had lived the life of a drudge. Her parents spoke very little, if any, English, and it is a tribute to their daughter's innate intelligence that she had learnt to speak English from the TV. When I met her, she was courageously waging a battle with her family to allow her younger sister to receive an education. Although they were still reluctant to allow the girl to go out to school, they were at least willing to bring tutors to the home. My friend, meanwhile, had enrolled in women-only adult-literacy classes and was busy making up for lost time.

This episode re-awoke in me the feelings of sorrow, anger and sheer incomprehension that I had felt years earlier when I met 'Shaheen' (not her real name) at university. Shaheen was a modern girl with short hair and a penchant for wearing badges bearing outrageous feminist slogans. She was an active and vocal member of the campus women's group and was rumoured to have links to the Southall Black Sisters.[1] Despite all this, she would often come and sit with the Muslim women students — there was a small group of us at the time, most of us wearing the hijab, and a good number of us were converts. Shaheen would interrogate us about our beliefs and why we had so willingly put on the hijab. At first, it felt like a typical feminist outburst, but I soon began to detect a lack of the vehemence that characterised other women's rights activists in the university and, curiously, a certain wistfulness. Something kept drawing her back to us.

Shaheen was from a Muslim background, and one day she told us a little about her childhood. Like thousands of other Asian children in Britain, she and her siblings had been sent to an extra-curricular Qur'an school every day after school, where they had spent hours learning to recite the Qur'an under the stern eye of the 'Mawlâna-Ṣâḥib'.[2] The slightest childish mistake or moment's inattention was likely to bring a blow from his stick and a torrent of harsh reprimands. Shaheen learnt, along with the other kids, how to recite the Qur'an parrot-fashion, but grew increasingly frustrated that she did not understand the words she was repeating endlessly. One day she asked her father, "But what does it mean?" Far from being pleased that his daughter was hoping to learn more about her religion, he beat her (the only time he ever hit his daughter) and told her in no uncertain terms never to ask such a question again, because such knowledge was only for boys and girls did not need to know it!

Such a harsh experience had a crushing impact on the little girl. Shaheen's ardent feminism clearly stemmed from this episode, and I felt that I could hardly blame her! Yet I could see that the fact that educated women had willingly turned their backs on their liberal WASP (White, Anglo-Saxon, Protestant) heritage and cheerfully donned the hijab was clearly giving her pause for thought. I lost touch with Shaheen soon after that, but I hope that our encounter showed her that Muslim women could also be educated women.

Depressing statistics

Sad to say, these stories are not atypical. On a global scale, educated Muslim women, even functionally literate women, are in the minority. At the beginning of the 1990s, it was glumly reported that a girl born in the Middle East or in South East Asia had less than one chance in three of completing primary education.[3] The dawn of the twenty-first century has not brought any great improvement in the statistics. In the majority of countries, women's literacy rates are still lower than those of men. Globally, according to a report by UNESCO, in 2008, two-thirds of the world's illiterate adults were women, and extremely low literacy rates are concentrated in three regions: South and West Asia, Sub-Saharan Africa and the Arab world.[4]

The statistics get even more depressing. Time after time, females in Muslim countries are shown to be losing out.[5] Fewer girls than boys are enrolled in school, and fewer women than men are literate. Blaming Islam for this state of affairs is too simplistic; similar disparities occur in other parts of the world that are predominantly non-Muslim as well, such as Latin America.[6] Other factors such as poverty, economic pressures, political unrest and so forth, also have a role to play. It is well known that even boys may not have the chance of a decent education when the labour of every family member is needed, from childhood onwards, just to enable the family to keep body and soul together. However, we cannot escape the fact that Islam is often (mis)used to justify denying education to girls, as in the two cases cited at the beginning of the chapter. There may even be a genuine, although misplaced, concern for the safety (moral and otherwise) of girls which compels parents to keep them home. But does Islam really demand of us that we lock up our daughters and keep them in ignorance?

Women's education at the time
of the Prophet (ﷺ)

To answer this question, we need to acquaint ourselves with how the Prophet (ﷺ) and his Companions dealt with the issue of women's education.

The very early days of Islam show us that women, smart, intelligent and knowledgeable, played a major role in the establishment of the new faith. Khadeejah (رضي الله عنها), the first convert to Islam, was a clever and capable woman who had dealt confidently with the outside world for years. She was aware of trends and issues in the society in which she lived, and was acquainted with the deep learning of her cousin Waraqah, to whom she took the Prophet (ﷺ) to hear words of verification and support following the first revelation. The account of 'Umar's sister attending a lesson in which the Qur'an was being taught indicates that women were taught equally with men from the beginning.

Later in Madinah, as the new Islamic society coalesced, we find the striking account of Asmâ' bint Yazeed, an Anṣâri woman who was delegated by the other women to ask an important question of the Prophet (ﷺ). She came to him when he was sitting with a group of his Companions (no sending questions on pieces of paper!) and put the women's question to him:

«O Prophet of Allah! You are dearer to me than my parents. The Muslim women have delegated me as their representative to speak to you on their behalf. Verily you are the Prophet of Allah for both men and women. We women stay, for the most part, within the four walls of our houses; we remain tied to our job of fulfilling the sexual desires of men, bearing children for them, and looking after their homes. Notwithstanding all this, men excel us in getting rewards for things which we are unable to do. They go and say their daily prayers and Friday congregational prayers in the mosque, visit the sick, attend funerals, perform hajj and, above all, fight in the way of Allah. When they go away for hajj or jihad, we look after their property, bring up their children and weave cloth for them. Do we not share a reward with them? The Prophet (ﷺ), addressing the Companions sitting with him, said: Did you ever hear a woman ask a better question? The Companions replied: O Prophet of Allah, we never thought that a lady could ever ask such a question. Addressing Asmâ', the Prophet (ﷺ) said: Listen carefully, and then go and tell the women who sent you that when a woman seeks the pleasure of her husband and carries out her domestic functions to his satisfaction, she gets the same reward as men get for all these services to Allah.»[7]

The Companions never thought that a woman could ask such a question (which may be a reflection of the misogynistic society from which Islam had recently rescued them). But the Prophet (ﷺ), far from telling women simply to put up with the situation, or to go away and stop asking impertinent questions, or denying her the opportunity to ask questions in the first place (all of which are likely to happen nowadays, in certain quarters!), expressed his admiration for the question, and took the time to provide a detailed answer.

Translators of the well-known hadith «Acquiring knowledge is a duty on every Muslim (*kulli Muslim*)»[8] often add the words "male or female" to make the point. Grammatically speaking, the words *kulli Muslim*, although masculine singular, convey the meaning of both male and female. The commandment is universal in application and, one might add, not only gender, but race, class or status are also irrelevant.

'Â'ishah (ﷺ), herself a leader in the field of education, praised the women of the Anṣâr for their enthusiasm for learning: "How good are the women of the Anṣâr that their shyness did not prevent them from learning and comprehending religious matters." This comment came when Asmâ' bint Yazeed was enquiring about ghusl (the ritual shower) following menstruation. She kept asking questions until she got answers, but when the Prophet (ﷺ) said that a woman should take a piece of cotton smeared with musk and cleanse herself, she asked how exactly this was to be done. The Prophet (ﷺ) felt too shy and respectful to spell it out; he said: «Praise be to Allah, cleanse yourself with it!» and covered his face. 'Â'ishah spoke quietly (according to another report, she took Asmâ' aside) and explained that she should apply the cotton to the traces of the blood that remained, that is, she should cleanse her private parts with it.[9] This report demonstrates how determined the first Muslim women were in their pursuit of knowledge. It also demonstrates some of the etiquette surrounding the teachings of more intimate aspects of ritual purification: it was not appropriate for the Prophet (ﷺ) to explain the details to a woman; the specific, intimate, information in this case was passed on from woman to woman.

The women were keen to seek religious knowledge, but were frustrated by the fact that the Prophet (ﷺ) was always surrounded by men. They asked him to set a day for them, which he did; he would teach them, and on occasion he would send someone on his behalf to teach them.[10]

Other examples of the importance placed on teaching women include the male converts who came to stay with the

Prophet (ﷺ) so that they could learn from him, and were subsequently told to go home and teach their wives and children what they had learned;[11] and the poor Companion who wanted to marry but could not afford a dowry and was told by the Prophet (ﷺ) to teach his bride whatever he knew of the Qur'an, and that would constitute the dowry.[12]

'Â'ishah (ﵠ): archetypical intellectual woman

'Â'ishah (ﵠ), of course, is the archetype of the intellectual woman in Islam. She narrated 2,210 hadiths[13] and was highly respected by male scholars, who would travel from afar to consult her. She was known as a fluent and eloquent speaker, and was adept in the fields of poetry, history, medicine and arithmetic[14], as well as the various fields of Islamic knowledge. She is known to have educated other women, such as 'Amrah bint 'Abdur-Rahmân, who narrated hadiths from her.

Other early Muslim women are also celebrated for their knowledge; among them we find the remarkable household of Umm Salamah. After her first husband died, the Prophet (ﷺ) married her, and cared for her children. Having lived in the household of the Prophet (ﷺ), not only were Umm Salamah and her daughter, Zaynab bint Abi Salamah, well-versed in knowledge, but her maid, Umm al-Hasan, was also known as an educated woman.[15]

Hafsah (ﵠ): custodian of the Qur'an

Let us not forget either that when it was decided to compile the Qur'an and ensure that it was preserved in writing, the precious leaves, shoulder-blades of camels, and so on, on which it had been written were entrusted to the care of a woman, Ḥafṣah bint 'Umar. Ḥafṣah had been taught to read and write by Shafa' bint 'Abdullâh, under the direction of the Prophet (ﷺ); she had also memorized the entire Qur'an. Shafa' had been one of only seventeen people of Quraysh (and the only woman among that number) who had been literate at the advent of Islam.[16]

Female scholars in history

Classical Islam is full of female scholars, seeking and conveying knowledge and working alongside their brothers in faith for the sake of furthering Islamic education. Even as late as the sixth century H. (the eleventh century C.E.), women were active on the academic scene in the Muslim world. They were involved in the field of Hadith science, amongst others, and numerous male scholars stated that they received their *ijâzah* (permission to narrate hadith) from these women; indeed, eminent scholars frequently mention women among their 'shaykhs' (scholarly teachers).[17] Many of these women came from scholarly families, and were the daughters of (and subsequently the wives of) scholars, as well as being scholars in their own right. One of the most fascinating of these stories is that of Fâṭimah bint Sa'd al-Khayr al-Anṣâri al-Andaloosi, who was born in China in 522 H. Her father had travelled from Spain to China — from one end of the Islamic world to the other! — in the service of knowledge. Although she was born in China, Fâṭimah was educated in Baghdad; her father and other great Hadith scholars were her teachers. She subsequently began her own teaching career, first in Damascus, then in Cairo, where she died in 600 H. She taught many scholars, including al-Mundhiri.[18]

The decline

What went wrong? As in the case of social restrictions, the deep-rooted bias against women reared its ugly head yet again and reaction against the revolutionary new measures brought by Islam took hold. The academic achievements referred to above took place in the second Abbasi period,[19] shortly before the Mongol onslaught that laid waste to so much of the Islamic world and destroyed cities and libraries (shed a tear for our lost heritage!). The following period (1250-1900) has been identified as the "centuries of decline"[20]; amidst the general devastation of society, women's rights deteriorated and women were to a great extent marginalized. With no public role, it was not thought important to educate them beyond, perhaps, the basics of their domestic duties and maybe a little religious information. Thus the vicious cycle began: uneducated mothers could not educate their daughters, and this pattern repeated itself through the centuries.[21]

This attitude that women did not need to be educated is reflected in a hadith attributed to 'Â'ishah (رضي) which says: "Do not house your women on upper floors, nor teach them reading or writing. Teach them to spin, and Soorat an-Noor." Hadith scholar, Shams al-Ḥaqq al-'Adheem Abâdi investigated this report and concluded that it is false, yet it has been repeatedly quoted by many scholars, which perhaps reflects the deep-rooted bias against women referred to above.[22]

In complete contrast to this, a sound report relates that the Prophet (ﷺ) asked a female companion, Shafa' bint 'Abdullâh, to teach a supplication to another woman: «Just as you have taught them reading (and writing) of the Book, will you not likewise teach them a supplication against skin allergies?» This indicates the Prophet's implicit approval of teaching writing to women.[23]

Selective education?

However, some scholars advise 'selective education' of women, especially in the face of widespread unemployment or underemployment among university graduates.[24] Writers constantly emphasise the maternal role as being primary, but the fact remains that there is a need, among Muslim communities world-wide, for more female teachers, doctors, nurses, social workers, and so forth. In particular, the Muslim girls' schools that are springing up in Western countries have an urgent need for female Muslim teachers, not only to satisfy religious/cultural needs surrounding segregation, but also to provide a positive role model for the girls themselves. We should also remember that there are women who are destined never to become mothers; far from marginalizing them and adding to their pain by emphasising the maternal role to the exclusion of all others, we must be aware that there have always been childless women in the Muslim community, and that their contribution in other fields has been invaluable — 'Â'ishah (ﷺ) being the primary example of this. In addition, there are plenty of wives and mothers who have the urge, and ability, to do more. As long as their family's needs are being adequately met, why should they not have the opportunity to do their part for the community?

There is no need, however, for Muslim women to storm the bastions of male-dominated work as is common nowadays in many Western countries; a male-dominated construction site is no place for a Muslim woman. In the summer of 1996, I met a sister at a conference whose training, prior to her embracing Islam, had led her into a male-dominated field. She had to work for economic reasons and was anxious to tell younger sisters not to follow her example. Fortunately, she had the strength of character to continue to wear the hijab and stick to her beliefs even in such an environment, but she regretted her career choice, and if she had had her time over again, would have done things very differently. There are, however, some fields that could benefit from more female input. Having lived in succession of homes that were impractical, awkward to clean, and otherwise appeared not to take the realities of family life into consideration, I can say that we could do with more female architects who might design homes for real people to live in! Women who have struggled to enter shops and board buses through doors that are too narrow for prams and strollers would also agree that perhaps female designers and engineers would be able to do a better job!

What do women need to know?

So, what should we teach girls? The very basics of education, which all people need, have been outlined in the following list of what literate women, of any background, should be able to do:

Read the labels on cans and boxes of food
Read a bus or train schedule
Look up numbers in a telephone directory
Read a contract, a health insurance form, a deed, or a waiver
Read a map
Read medical directions
Help their children with homework
Read the menu in a restaurant
Read road signs
Get a job requiring reading or writing
Read the warning labels on poisons and pesticides
Read a letter from a relative or friend and write a response
Keep their own accounts.[25]

This list should be self-explanatory. In the case of mothers, who are the primary-givers for their children, being able to understand simple medical instructions may even be a matter of life and death. For Muslims living in non-Muslim countries, being able to read food labels is important for pork detection purposes. I have seen, in Muslim kitchens, products that are clearly labelled as containing lard! Muslims need to be able to read the labels, and to know what things such as lard are (pork and its by-products go by many names); this is basic knowledge that is essential to ensure that what they buy is *ḥalâl*.[26] Furthermore, in the 21st century, computer literacy has become almost as essential as basic literacy, as filling out e-forms is a frequent requirement in many routine transactions. For a woman who rarely leaves her home, access to knowledge and information over the Internet can help her to continue her own education in her religion and in other fields of interest.

In addition to functional literacy, Muslims need at least the basic Islamic knowledge that will enable them, for example, to pray and fast properly. They also need an understanding of ritual purity (which for women extends to at least a basic understanding of their bodies and natural cycles). These are the very basics; girls should also be equipped and empowered to read for themselves so that they can increase their own knowledge.

Arabic should also be taught, not just parrot-fashion as in the old-fashioned Qur'an schools, but as a language. In addition, translations of the Qur'an should be made available in the local language so that some understanding may be gained.

This is the minimum education that should be available to Muslim girls and women. No Muslim woman should ever be discouraged or prevented from reaching her full potential. There is a wealth of talent and ability that should not be wasted.

Can women travel to seek knowledge?

An interesting opinion on women's seeking knowledge was provided by Dr. Darsh of London, England. In response to a query about whether a woman may leave home without a maḥram in search of worldly knowledge, he referred to the restrictions on women's travel given in hadiths, which state that a woman may not travel "the distance of three nights or one day and one night" without a maḥram. Dr. Darsh points out that at that time, people would travel alone through the desert, and women in particular would be in danger of being harmed. In contrast, people nowadays tend to travel within large groups, as in a bus or plane, "as though a whole village is on the move together", which affords some protection to women travellers. Muslim women can always find others to travel with and stay with at their destination.[27] When I was a student, I lived for a while in a hostel for Muslim women students in London where, despite the inherent aggravations of communal living, I had the opportunity to live with sisters from all over the world, and had a measure of security and the freedom to learn and practice my new faith. Such hostels are an excellent idea, especially when so many Muslim women are travelling to other cities and countries in search of knowledge.

How to educate our daughters

Having determined that Muslim girls should be educated, we should give some thought to the question of where and how this may be achieved. There are four main options, which we will look at briefly:

1. <u>Home-schooling</u>: This is an increasingly popular choice among Muslim parents in the West. You do not need to have a PhD in education, but you should have an abundance of patience and stamina, enthusiasm for learning (to provide a positive role model), and a sense of initiative. Usually, one parent commits herself/himself to home-schooling full-time. This requires at least a basic level of education, but many home-schoolers find themselves learning along with their children. You may have to deal with the local education authority or board of education, and satisfy them that your children are being adequately educated. This may involve drawing up a syllabus and keeping records to demonstrate what you are doing. Home-schooling organisations exist in many countries, and you can get help with the legal side of things. There are also Muslim parents who have been quietly home-schooling for years: this is a general plea to them to share the fruits of their experience for the benefit of others.

2. <u>Islamic schools</u>: The number of Islamic schools is increasing, especially for girls (which begs the question: what about the boys?). It is good to have an Islamic atmosphere, some formal instruction in Islamic religion, history and culture, and the opportunity to participate in daily prayers. It is also a relief not to have to worry about Christmas/Hallowe'en/Easter, mixed sports lessons, sex education classes that do not reflect moral teachings, and kids being taught how to dance the macarena! However, parents cannot relax completely: some Islamic schools give the impression of being 'ethnic ghettoes' where the ethos is more that of a particular ethnic or linguistic group than of a universal Islam. I have even heard of 'love-notes' being passed back and forth between supposedly segregated boys and girls in another school. The fact that Islamic schools are private and hence charge tuition is also a barrier to many families. Islamic schools

are to be encouraged, but we must avoid the pitfalls surrounding them.

3. <u>Private schools</u>: Many private schools in Western countries are single-sex, which is the attraction for Muslim parents. However, a girls' school may be affiliated with a boys' school and there may be some joint activities, so segregation is far from total. Payment of expensive fees is no guarantee of excellence, either moral or academic. Many private schools have a specifically Christian ethos; this raises issues regarding religious education and church attendance, which may be compulsory.

4. <u>Public (state) schools</u>: This is the 'choice' of the majority of Muslim parents living in the West, most of whom have no other choice! Public schooling raises many issues and concerns, but there are ways to lessen the negative impact. Parents can shop around for the best school in their locality. It may not be the nearest school, and travel time to and from the school may be longer, but it will be worth it. Muslim parents from all backgrounds should join together and present a united front over issues of concern; they should also offer alternative suggestions, and be prepared to get involved and help to implement any such alternatives. Muslim parents are not alone: there are already organisations that have experience in dealing with such matters, and which can be contacted for information and advice.[28]

Summary

Although current statistics and anecdotal evidence about the level of women's education make for depressing reading, they do not reflect true Islamic values. Islam enjoins the teaching of both male and female, not just the basics of Islamic knowledge, but all areas of beneficial knowledge. This is clearly reflected in the example of the Prophet (ﷺ) and the women of Madinah and classical Islam, where women were recognised for their knowledge in medicine, literature, and so on, as well as Islamic knowledge. The need exists today for educated Muslim women as teachers, doctors, nurses, midwives, school workers, lawyers, and so forth. The need exists wherever there are Muslim communities. We must not repress our daughters in the name of Islam; we have to ensure that they receive an education that covers Islamic as well as other areas of knowledge. Educated Muslim women also have a responsibility to teach their sisters and be a role model for younger females; 'each one teach one' is a slogan we may adopt, and pass on whatever knowledge we have to our sisters, whether formally or informally. Whatever kind of schooling we choose for our daughters (and sons), the most important thing we can do for them is to set the example at home, in teaching them correct Islamic behaviour and morals, and above all an awareness of Allah (ﷻ), so that when they venture forth into the world they will be equipped to make their own, informed, Islamic choices, inshâ' Allâh.

Notes

Chapter 1

[1] *hijab* (*ḥijâb*): veil ordained by Allah (the Exalted) for Muslim women

[2] Ibn Katheer, *Tafseer al-Qur'an al-Adheem*, vol. 1, p. 537

[3] *taqwâ*: fearful awareness of Allah; being mindful of Allah; pious dedication; being careful not to transgress the bounds set by Allah

[4] Aminah Wadud-Muhsin, *Qur'an and Woman*, p. 73 (referring to Sayyid Quṭb, *Fee Dhilâl al Qur'an*)

[5] Afzular Rahman, *Role of Muslim Woman in Society*, pp. 250-251

[6] Maulana Abul A'ala Mawdudi, *The Laws of Marriages and Divorce in Islam*, p. 17

[7] An interesting hadith narrated in *Ṣaheeh Muslim* describes the leader of an armed expedition lighting a fire and commanding his men to enter it. Some were prepared to obey, others refused. When the Prophet (bpuh) heard of it, he commended those who had disobeyed orders and said: «There is no obedience in disobedience to Allah. Obedience is only in what is right.» (*Ṣaheeh Muslim, Kitâb al-Imârah*, vol. 3, p. 1022; this translation is taken from Kaukab Siddique, *The Struggle of Muslim Women*, p. 26 ff.)

[8] e.g. Wadud-Muhsin, op. cit., p. 68; Rahman, op. cit., p. 253

[9] Wadud-Muhsin, op. cit., p. 68

[10] Abdullah Yusuf Ali, *The Meaning of the Holy Qur'an* (Translation and Commentary), note 255

[11] See Rahman, op. cit., pp. 254-255, where the author ties this in to the importance (and complications) of genealogy.

[12] Yusuf Ali, note 2201

[13] Yusuf Ali, note 4621

[14] Some may agree that this verse is not talking about how women 'should' be, but argue that it is describing how women actually are. The author's explanation does not address that question, which may be in the minds of many people, i.e., why does the Qur'an describe women as trivial-minded beings concerned with trinkets and who cannot express themselves plainly? (Editor)

[15] *'umrah*: a minor, non-obligatory pilgrimage to Makkah

[16] *ghusl*: ritual shower necessary after a major impurity, e.g., after sexual intercourse or at the end of the menstrual period

[17] *wuḍoo'*: ablution required before prayer or touching the Qur'an

[18] *Tafseer al-Jalâlayn*, p. 47

[19] *Ṣaḥeeḥ Muslim, Kitâb aṭ-Ṭahârah*, vol. 1, p. 175. The symbols «...» are used in this book to enclose the translated text of an authentic hadith.

[20] *Ṣaḥeeḥ al-Bukhari, Kitâb al-Hayḍ*, vol. 1, p. 179; *Ṣaḥeeḥ Muslim, Kitâb aṭ-Ṭahârah*, vol. 1, p. 175

[21] Philips, B., Islamic Rules on Menstruation & Post-Natal Bleeding, 2nd ed., Riyadh: International Islamic Publishing House 2005, pp. 20-21 & f.n. 14

[22] Eid (*'eed*): lit. festival; the two celebrations: one at the end of Ramadan and the other at the culmination of the Hajj

[23] *takbeerât*: the act of repeatedly saying 'Allâhu Akbar' and other phrases praising Allah

[24] *Sunan Abi Dâwood*, Book 1, no. 0212

Chapter 2

[1] The description of marriage as "half the faith" is derived from the hadith: «When a servant of Allah marries, he has completed half of his religious obligations, and he must fear Allah in order to complete the second half.» (Al-Bayhaqi)

[2] Khansa' bint Khiḍam al-Anṣâriyah narrated that her father gave her away in marriage when she was a matron, and she disliked that marriage. So she went to Allah's Messenger (bpuh) and he declared that marriage invalid. *Ṣaḥeeḥ al-Bukhâri*, vol. 7, p. 52

[3] See list of suggested questions — Appendix 1

[4] Although the idea of considering class appears to be contrary to the Islamic ideal of egalitarianism, the scholars recognised the reality of human societies and the almost universal urge of people to stratify themselves. As Hammudah Abdul 'Ati points out, the early Muslim conquests brought Islam to regions where urban civilisation was long-established and society was highly stratified. In addition, "the native converts had not themselves directly experienced the sense of religious cohesiveness and social levelling of the early Muslim community." (*The Family Structure in Islam*, p. 92). The rulings and advice of the scholars are clearly reactions to the social reality that they encountered. (See: Hammudah Abdul 'Ati, *The Family Structure in Islam*, pp. 94-97)

[5] *Sunnah*: the practice and collected sayings of Prophet Muhammad (bpuh) that together with the Qur'an forms the basis of Islamic law

[6] See *Soorat al-Baqarah (Qur'an 2: 229-230)*

[7] Abdur Rahman I Doi, *Woman in Shari'ah*, p. 92ff

[8] Abul A'ala Mawdudi, *The Laws of Marriage and Divorce in Islam*, pp. 30-31; Abdur Rahman I Doi, *Woman in Shari'ah*, p. 85

[9] Sayyid Sabiq, *Fiqh as-Sunnah* (Arabic), vol. 8, p. 142ff

[10] Thâbit's wife — hadith reported by Bukhari and al-Bayhaqi. See also Abdur Rahman I Doi, *Woman in Shari'ah*, p. 97

[11] Afzular Rahman, *Role of Muslim Woman in Society*, p. 153ff

[12] Abdur Rahman I Doi, *Woman in Shari'ah*, p. 98

[13] Abdul 'Ati, op. cit., p. 239

[14] *Ummah*: community or nation: *usu.* used to refer to the entire global community of Muslims

Chapter 3

[1] Roti, kibbeh and melokhia are names of traditional dishes in certain Muslim countries. (Editor)

[2] Dr. S. M. Darsh, letter to author

[3] *mahram*: a degree of consanguinity precluding marriage; a man whom a woman may never marry due to the close blood or marriage relationship. e.g., father, brother, son, uncle, and father-in-law

[4] Dr. S. M. Darsh, letter to author

[5] Dr. S. M. Darsh, letter to author

[6] Dr. S. M. Darsh, letter to author

[7] Dr. S. M. Darsh, letter to author

[8] Ramadan: the month of obligatory fasting; the ninth month of the Hijri calendar

[9] *iftâr*: the meal eaten at sunset to break the fast

[10] *suhoor*: the pre-dawn meal eaten before the start of a fasting day

[11] *tarâweeh*: special communal night prayers performed only in Ramadan

[12] *maghrib*: sunset, the obligatory prayer at that time

[13] *'ishâ'*: evening; the obligatory prayer at that time

[14] *fajr*: dawn; the obligatory prayer at that time

[15] *juz'* (pl. *ajzâ'*): a section of the Qur'an equal to one thirtieth of the text; the Qur'an may thus be divided in order to complete reading the whole text in the 30 days of Ramadan

[16] Umm Abdullah, "Ramadan: Work or Pray?" in *Usra — The Muslim Family Magazine*, no. 43, Ramadan 1412 A.H. / March 1992

[17] Akhlaq Husain, *Muslim Parents: Their Rights and Duties*, p. 80

[18] Muslim

[19] M. Qutb, *Women Around the Messenger*, 2007, pp. 254 ff.

[20] Akhlaq Husain, op. cit., p. 83

[21] Khurshid Ahmad, *Foreword* to Anis Ahmed: *Muslim Women and Higher Education: A Case for Separate Institutions for Women.*

[22] See: *Handbook of Contraceptive Practices*, (UK) Department of Health, p. 43; *Mother & Baby Magazine*, September 1992, p. 107. (This information was originally supplied by Mrs. Victoria Gillick). See also: The Boston Women's Health Collective, *The New Our Bodies Ourselves*, p. 250.

[23] The rapid increase in the use of the pill in the 1960s, when it had not even been fully tested, has been described as a "gigantic experiment" (*The New Our Bodies Ourselves*, p. 237). Important note: Whilst this book contains much useful health information, the authors' stance on morality issues differs markedly from Islamic views. Quoting health information from this source is in no way to be seen as endorsing the book's stance on abortion, sexuality, etc.

[24] See: Alia Schleifer, *Motherhood in Islam*, p. 7ff

[25] Christine Davidson, *Staying Home Instead: Alternatives to the Two-Paycheck Family.*

[26] Mary Ann Cahill, *The Heart Has Its Own Reasons: An Inspirational Resource Guide for Mothers Who Choose to Stay Home with Their Young Children.*

Chapter 4

[1] Jan Goodwin, *Price of Honor*, p. 190ff

[2] Jan Goodwin, *Price of Honor*, p. 197

[3] See *Islamic Sisters International*, vol. 3, no. 1, Jun/Jul 1994, p. 3

[4] This very real anecdote was provided by a sister who knew the family well, but who of course wishes to preserve their anonymity and thus their privacy.

[5] Abdur Rahman Doi, *Woman in Shariah*, p. 60ff

[6] A true story, told to the author by a relative of the gentleman in question

[7] For a further discussion of the issue of justice and fairness in plural marriages, see Philips and Jones, op. cit., chapter 4 "Division in Plural marriages".

[8] *Islamic Sisters International*, vol. 3, no. 2, Aug-Oct 1994, p. 31

[9] Bilal Philips and Jameelah Jones, *Polygamy in Islam*, p. 82

[10] Bilal Philips and Jameelah Jones, *Polygamy in Islam*, p. 82

[11] *kâfir*: lit. 'unbeliever'; non-Muslim

[12] *Islamic Sisters International*, vol. 2, no. 4, October 1993, p. 3

[13] Dr. S. M. Darsh, letter to author.

[14] *Islamic Sisters International*, vol. 3, no. 2, Aug/Oct 1994, p. 19

[15] Al-Mundhiri's explanation was translated and provided to the author in a letter to her by Dr. Suhayb Hasan.

[16] Dr. S. M. Darsh, "What You Ought To Know", Q news, 7-14 April, 1995

[17] Hadith narrated by 'Â'ishah (ﷺ): «Allah's Messenger (ﷺ) used to divide his time equally amongst us and would pray: O Allah, this is my division in what I possess, so please do not hold me to blame for the division (of affection) which only You control.» See Bilal Philips & Jameelah Jones, *Polygamy in Islam*, p. 52

[18] Maryam Jameelah — an American convert and author of a number of books

[19] A number of accounts written by co-wives describe such close, warm and supportive relationships within plural marriages; other co-wives are described as accepting their situation, but choose not to interact so closely with one another. See *Islamic Sisters International*, vol. 3, no. 1, (June/July 1994) and vol. 3, no. 2, (Aug/Oct 1994).

[20] Umm Qaseem (Joy Henderson), "My Parents Sold Me to my Husband", *Islamic Sisters International*, vol. 3, no. 1, (June/July 1994) and vol. 3, no. 2, (Aug/Oct 1994)

Chapter 5

[1] Muslim Women's Help Line (London, England), Annual Report, 1994.

[2] MWHL Annual Report, 1994

[3] "Forum", *Islamic Sisters International*, vol. 2, no. 4, p. 5, 10, October 1993

[4] MWHL Annual Report, 1994; "I am a Woman, hear me ROAR", p. 3; *Islamic Sisters International*, vol. 2, no. 4, p. 5, 10, October 1993

[5] "I am a Woman, hear me ROAR", p. 3; *Islamic Sisters International*, vol. 2, no. 4, pp. 5 & 10, October 1993

[6] Aminah Wadud-Muhsin, *Qur'an and Woman*, p. 76

[7] Yusuf al-Qaradawi, *The Lawful and the Prohibited in Islam*, p. 205-207

[8] Bukhari, Kitâb an-Nikâḥ; Aḥmad

[9] Aḥmad, Abu Dâwood and an-Nisâ'i

[10] Muslim and an-Nisâ'i

[11] Wadud-Muhsin, op. cit., p. 76
[12] Wadud-Muhsin, op. cit., p. 76
[13] Afzular Rahman, *Role of Muslim Woman in Society*, p. 413ff
[14] *Islamic Sisters International*, vol. 2, no. 4, October 1993 (Special issue on spouse abuse)
[15] Mohammad Raza, *Islam in Britain*, pp. 100-101
[16] Women's Aid Federation of England: *Breaking Through: Women Surviving Male Violence*, p. 84
[17] MWHL Annual Report, 1994
[18] Shanaz Khan, thesis, OISE/UT (Ontario Institute for Studies in Education / University of Toronto): the cases referred to happened in Toronto, Canada.
[19] Bukhari
[20] "Forum" pp. 5 & 10; *Islamic Sisters International*, vol. 2, no. 4, pp. 5 & 10, October 1993
[21] Bukhari, *Kitâb an-Nikâḥ*
[22] Muslim, *Kitâb ar-Riḍâ'*
[23] Muslim
[24] See Kaukab Siddique, *The Struggle of Muslim Women*, p. 28
[25] Muslim, *Kitâb an-Nikâḥ*
[26] The translation of the Arabic adjective *a'waj* here is given as 'bent', but it can just as accurately be translated as 'curved', which is a word that does not have the negative connotations of 'bent'. In fact, the well-known da'wah preacher Amr Khaled uses this interpretation, and has said that the rib is curved because it has a very important function: to protect the heart it encircles. (Editor)

Chapter 6

[1] *Tarbiyah* is an important concept in Islam. Although the word is often translated as 'education', it goes beyond the three R's [reading, writing and (a)rithmetic] and encompasses moral and spiritual teaching. Tarbiyah also involves a strong element of character building, moral education and self-discipline, so "holistic education" may be a good approximation to the meaning of the word.
[2] Dr. S.M. Darsh, letter to author
[3] Dr. S.M. Darsh, letter to author
[4] One such case is described in a letter sent to *Islamic Sisters International* in response to their special issue on spousal abuse, proving that abuse can go

both ways. In this case, the wife initially agreed to an Islamic upbringing for the children, but under pressure from her parents began to take them to church and teach them Christianity; eventually the marriage ended in a bitter divorce and at the time of this writing, this brother has not seen his children for years (*Islamic Sisters International*, vol. 3, no. 2, Aug/Oct 1994)

[5] Sayyid Abul A'la Mawdudi, *Witnesses Unto Mankind: The Purpose and Duty of the Muslim Ummah*, p. 20

[6] Yusuf al-Qaradawi, *The Lawful and the Prohibited in Islam*, p. 335

[7] Dr. S.M. Darsh, letter to author

[8] *minbar*: raised pulpit in a mosque from which sermons are presented

Chapter 7

[1] See e.g. Jamal Badawi, *The Muslim Women's Dress According to the Qur'an and Sunnah*

[2] jilbâb: a long, loose coat worn to cover a woman's indoor clothing, as part of her hijab

[3] See Abu Bilal Mustafa al-Kanadi, *The Islamic Ruling Regarding Women's Dress According to the Qur'an and Sunnah*, for a discussion on various scholarly viewpoints.

[4] Ṣaḥeeḥ al-Bukhâri, Kitâb al-'Eedayn, vol. 2, p. 52

[5] Lamya al-Faruqi, *Women, Muslim Society and Islam*, p. 13

[6] Al-Faruqi, 1988, p. 6

[7] Dr. S. M. Darsh, letter to author; see also Albert Hourani's *A History of the Arab Peoples* (Warner, 1991) for a detailed exploration of this historically-documented social phenomenon. (Editor)

[8] Loise Cainker, "Palestinian-American Muslim Women: Living on the Margins of Two Worlds," in Earle H. Waugh et al (eds.), *Muslim Families in North America*, p. 291ff.

[9] Mohammad S. Raza, *Islam in Britain*, p. 3

[10] This book (*Ideal Woman in Islam* by Muhammad Imran) was given to me when I was a very, very new convert and had barely begun to explore women's issues in Islam. It was the cause of much alarm! Later I was able to see that it is aimed at Muslim women living in Pakistan, a very different audience than that of newly-converted Muslims from a Western background.

[11] Muhammad Imran, *Ideal Woman in Islam*, p. 88

[12] Imran, pp. 115-116

[13] Chapman, James "Two-thirds of hospitals failing to meet Government pledge to end mixed-sex wards". *Daily Mail*, 19 May 2008.

[14] Cahill, 1983

[15] Davidson, 1993

[16] Aminah Wadud-Muhsin, *Qur'an and Woman*, p. 98

[17] See hadiths in *Ṣaḥeeḥ al-Bukhâri, Kitâb al-'Eedayn*, vol. 2, pp. 50ff and *Kitâb al-'Ilm*, vol. 1, p. 78

[18] *Ṣaḥeeḥ al-Bukhâri*, op. cit.

[19] M. Qutb, *Women Around the Messenger*, International Islamic Publishing House, 2007

[20] Muhammad Iqbal Siddiqui, *Islam Forbids Free Mixing of Men and Women*, p. 71

[21] M. Qutb, *Women Around the Messenger*, International Islamic Publishing House, 2007

[22] *da'wah*: disseminating the teachings of Islam and calling on people to accept and embrace Islam

[23] For further discussions of these issues, see Dr. Hassan Al Turabi's groundbreaking 1973 article, *Women in Islam and Muslim Society*, that has been translated into English and made available on the Internet. (Editor)

Chapter 8

[1] "Girl's death leads to ban", *Al Ahram Weekly*, issue no. 852, 5-11 July, 2007

[2] Badawi, *Gender Equity in Islam*, Appendix

[3] Clinical definitions adapted from Scilla McLean and Stell Efua Graham, *Female Circumcision, Excision and Infibulation*, p. 3

[4] Al-Nafisah, "Female Circumcision and Islam", Contemporary Jurisprudence Research Journal, Riyadh

[5] McLean and Graham 1995, p. 3

[6] *harâm*: forbidden according to Islamic law

[7] McLean and Graham, p. 6

[8] Nawal Saadawi, *Hidden Face of Eve*, p. 40

[9] Information from ISSRA (Islamic Social Services Resources Association), Toronto.

[10] Saadawi, op. cit., p. 7ff.

[11] Boddy, *Wombs and Alien Spirits: Women, Men and the Zar Cult in Northern Sudan*, p. 51

[12] Boddy, 1989, p. 51

[13] Janie Hampton, "Going to Grannie's", *New Internationalist*, February 1993, pp. 16-17

[14] Hampton, 1993

[15] Dr. S.M. Darsh, letter to author

[16] Bukhari, vol. 1, chapter 29, p. 174 ff.

[17] Dr. Muhammad Salim al-Awwa, *Islamic Ruling on Male and Female Circumcision: Female Circumcision Neither a Sunna, nor a Sign of Respect*, 2007

[18] Dr. Suhayb Hasan, letter to author

[19] At-Ṭabarâni and Al-Ḥâkim, Abu Dâwood, who classified it as weak, due to an unknown narrator in its chain. According to Hadith scholars, this hadith is transmitted via three different chains, all of them defective, thus it cannot be considered an authentic hadith. (Editor)

[20] Al-Awwa, M. *Islamic Ruling on Male and Female Circumcision: Neither a Sunna, Nor a Sign of Respect*

[21] Badawi, J., 2001, op. cit.

[22] Boddy, op. cit., p. 53

[23] Saadawi, op. cit., p. 42

[24] See also: Abdullah Hakim Quick, "Muslims must trash backward practices", *Toronto Star*, Sept. 7, 1996.

[25] Abudullah Hakim Quick, "Islamic Perspective on Cultural Practices", speech given at ISSRA Conference on Health and Social Issues, Toronto, May 25, 1996

[26] Boston Women's Health Collective, *Our Bodies Our Selves*, p. 617

[27] Hampton, op. cit.

[28] Boddy, op. cit., p. 52

Chapter 9

[1] An 'anti-fundamentalist' feminist group which was active in London, England in the 1980s. Southall is a London suburb that is home to many Asian families, including a large number of Muslims. For some unfathomable reason, in Britain anyone who is not "white" is therefore regarded as being "Black"!

[2] An honorary title of a religious teacher in Urdu/Hindi

[3] Marcela Ballara, *Women and Literacy*, p. 17

4 UN News Centre, "Global progress in literacy masks sharp regional gaps, UN report finds", 8 October 2008. http://www.un.org/apps/news/story.asp?NewsID=28447&Cr=literacy&Cr1= Accessed Dec. 2008

5 Robin Morgan (ed), *Sisterhood is Global*, passim; see also the annual UNESCO Statistical Yearbook

6 Morgan, 1995

7 Hadith narrated by Aḥmad; translation adopted from Muhammad Imran, *Ideal Woman in Islam*, p. 50

8 Ibn Mâjah (this is a weak hadith, but An-Nawawi said that its meaning was true)

9 *Ṣaḥeeḥ Muslim, Kitâb al-Ḥayḍ*, vol. 1, p. 188

10 Abdur Rahman I. Doi, *Woman in Shari'ah*, p. 138; *Ṣaḥeeḥ al-Bukhâri, Kitâb al-'Ilm*, vol. 1, p. 80ff.

11 Afzular Rahman, *Role of Muslim Woman in Society*, p. 107; Doi, op. cit., p. 139

12 Doi, op. cit., p. 139

13 Allama Saiyid Sulayman Nadvi, *Hazrat Ayesha Siddiqa*, p. 60

14 Rahman, op. cit., p. 57; Nadvi, op. cit., p. 85

15 Rahman, op. cit., p. 57

16 Nadvi, op. cit., p. 9

17 Muhammad al-Ghazâli, *Turâthuna al-Fikri [Our Intellectual Heritage]*, p. 158 ff.

18 Muhammad al-Ghazâli, *Turâthuna al-Fikri*, p. 163.

19 Al-Ghazâli, p. 158

20 Lamya al-Faruqi, *Women, Muslim Society and Islam*, p. 11

21 Dr. S.M. Darsh, *Islam and the Education of Muslim Women* (unpublished paper)

22 Darsh, op. cit.

23 Darsh, op. cit.; also Rahman, op. cit., p. 108

24 Darsh, op. cit.

25 Ballara, op. cit., p. 59

26 *halal (ḥalâl)*: permitted according to Islamic law

27 Dr. S.M. Darsh, "What You Ought To Know" in *Q news*, January, 6, 1995

28 In Western countries, a number of Muslim organisations are working both with Muslim families and education professionals. See Appendix 2 for a brief list.

Bibliography

'Abd al-'Ati, Hammudah, *The Family Structure in Islam*, American Trust Publications, 1977

Ahmad, Anis, *Muslim Women and Higher Education: A Case for Separate Institutions for Women*, Islamabad: Institute of Policy Studies (2nd rev. edn.)

Ṣaḥeeḥ al-Bukhâri: See Khan

Badawi, Jamal A., *Aṭ-Ṭaḥârah: Purity and State of Undefilement* Plainfield, Indiana: Islamic Teaching Centre / American Trust Publications, 1979

_____ , *The Muslim Woman's Dress According to the Qur'an and Sunnah*, London: Ta-Ha Publications, 1980

_____ , *Gender Equity in Islam*, Washington, DC: Islamic Affairs Department, 2001

Ballara, Marcela, *Women and Literacy*, London, Zed Books, 1992

Boddy, Janice, *Wombs and Alien Spirits: Women, Men and the Zar Cult in Northern Sudan*, Madison, Wisconsin: The University of Wisconsin Press, 1989

Cahill, Mary Ann., *The Heart Has Its Own Reasons: An Inspirational Resource Guide for Mothers Who Choose to Stay Home with Their Young Children*, New York: Plume/New American Library, 1983

Davidson, Christine, *Staying Home Instead: Alternatives to the Two-Paycheck Family*, New York: Lexington Books, 1993 (rev. ed.)

Doi, Abdur Rahman, *Woman in Shari'ah*, London: Ta-Ha Publications, 1989

Al-Faruqi, Lamya, *Women, Muslim Society and Islam*, Indianopolis: American Trust Publications, 1988

Hourani, Albert, *A History of the Arab Peoples*, New York: Warner Books, 1991

Husain, Akhlaq, *Muslim Parents: Their Rights and Duties*, New Delhi: Adam Publishers and Distributors, 1985 (2nd ed.)

Ibn Katheer, 'Imad al-Deen Abi al-Fida' Ismail, *Tafseer al-Qur'an al-'Azeem*, Riyadh: Maktabah Dar as-Salaam, 1992

Al-Kanadi, Abu Bilal Mustafa, *The Islamic Ruling Regarding Women's Dress According to the Qur'an and Sunnah*, Jeddah: Abul Qasim Publishing House, 1991

Khan, Dr. Muhammad Muhsin, *The Translation of the Meanings of Ṣaḥeeḥ al-Bukhâri*, New Delhi: Kitab Bhavan, 1987 (rev. ed.)

Mawdudi, Sayyid Abul A'la, *Witnesses unto Mankind: The Purpose and Duty of the Muslim Ummah*, Leicester: The Islamic Foundation, 1986

McLean, Scilla & Graham, Stell Efua (eds.), *Female Circumcision, Excision and Infibulation: The Facts and Proposals for Change*, London: Minority Rights Group, 1985 (2nd. rev. ed.)

Morgan, Robin (ed.), *Sisterhood is Global: The International Women's Movement Anthology*, New York: Anchor Books, 1984

Nadvi, Allama Saiyid Salaiman, *Hazrat Ayesha Siddiqa: Her Life and Works*, Kuwait: Islamic Book Publishers, 1993 (2nd ed.)

Philips, Abu Ameenah Bilal, *Islamic Rules on Menstruation & Post-Natal Bleeding*, 2nd ed., Riyadh: International Islamic Publishing House, 2005

Philips, Abu Ameenah Bilal & Jones, Jameelah, *Polygamy in Islam*, Riyadh: (IIPH) International Islamic Publishing House, 2006

Al-Qaradawi, Yusuf, *The Lawful and the Prohibited in Islam (al-Halal wal Haram fil Islam)*, London: Shorouk International, 1985

Qutb, Muhammad 'Ali, *Women Around the Messenger*, Riyadh: International Islamic Publishing House, 2007

Qutb, Sayyid, *Fee Dhilal al-Qur'an* [In the Shade of the Qur'an], Beirut: Dar al-Shuruq, 1980

Rahman, Afzular, *Role of Muslim Women in Society*, London: Seerah Foundations, 1986

Raza, Muhammad S., *Islam in Britain: Past, Present and the Future*, Leicester: Volcano Press, 1991

El-Sayed, Mohamed, "Girl's death leads to ban", *Al Ahram Weekly*, issue no. 852, 5-11 July, 2007

Sabiq, al-Sayyid, *Fiqh as-Sunnah*, Egypt: Maktabat al-Adab, n.d.

Schleifer, Aliah, *Motherhood in Islam*, Cambridge: The Islamic Academy, 1986

Siddiqi, Muhammad Iqbal, *Islam Forbids Free Mixing of Men and Women*, Lahore: Kazi Publications, 1983

Siddique, Kaukab, *Liberation of Women Thru [sic] Islam*, Kingsville, MD: American Society for Education and Religion, Inc., 1990

_____, *The Struggle of Muslim Women*, Dhaka: Jamaat al-Muslimeen Bangladesh, 1994

United Nations, *Women: Challenges to the Year 2000*, New York: United Nations, 1991

Wadud-Muhsin, Aminah, *Qur'an and Woman*, Kuala Lampur: Penerbit Fajar Bakti Sdn. Bhd., 1992 (3rd imp. 1994)

Waugh, Earle H. et al. (eds.), *Muslim Families in North America*, Edmonton: The University of Alberta Press, 1991

Women's Aid Federation England Ltd. (W.A.F.E.), *Breaking Through: Women Surviving Male Violence*, Bristol, UK: W.A.F.E., c.1989

On the Web:

Al Turabi, Hassan, *Women in Islam and Muslim Society*, 1973
http://www.islamfortoday.com/turai01.htm
Last accessed December 2008

Chapman, James, 'Two-thirds of hospitals failing to meet Government pledge to end mixed-sex wards', *Daily Mail*, 19 May 2008.
http://www.dailymail.co.uk/news/article-1020529/Two-thirds-hospitals-failing-meet-Government-pledge-end-mixed-sex-wards.html
Last accessed Jan. 2009

Islam for Today, website run by Shaykh Salman al-Oudeh: www.islamfortoday.com

UN News Centre, "Global progress in literacy masks sharp regional gaps, UN report finds", 8 October 2008.
http://www.un.org/apps/news/story.asp?NewsID=28447&Cr=literacy&Cr1=
Accessed Dec. 2008

APPENDIX ONE

Questions to ask a prospective husband

*W*hen choosing a partner, there are numerous issues that may lead to friction and conflict. Following the principle that prevention is better than cure, it seems wise to air these issues before a match is finalised. Some of the issues may appear trivial or mundane, but the stuff of everyday life is also the stuff of arguments! Other issues are more serious and may be indicative of the potential for a stormy and abusive marriage. Each marriage will have its ups and downs, but settling some of these matters may avoid the emergence of major, insoluble problems and consequent heartbreak.

These are all questions that may be asked directly or else 'researched' by observation, asking his relatives, members of the community, and so on. The prospective bride may ask some of these questions when the couple meet, but many women may feel too shy to ask outright. Family and friends can also help with the research. In many Muslim countries, relatives of prospective partners often visit to check the person out.

Asking/answering such questions is not considered backbiting, and people should not hesitate to tell the truth when it concerns a possible marriage; the intent is to establish whether these two people are compatible. Avoiding a poor match will save all concerned from much heartache. At the same time, whether the marriage proceeds or not, any information thus gathered should be kept confidential; any 'faults' uncovered should not be generally broadcast in the community!

These suggested questions are derived from two sources: an article entitled "Spousal Abuse and its Prevention" by Br. Abdul Rahman in *Islamic Sisters International*,[1] and the feedback I received during a workshop I led on "Choosing A Marriage Partner" at the ISSRA Conference on Health and Social Issues, Toronto, May 25, 1996.

The big issues

1. What makes him angry and how does he deal with his anger?

Does he blame everybody but himself?
Does he stop talking to the person involved?
Does he bear grudges ("I will get back one day!")
Has he ever physically or mentally abused anyone with whom he was angry?
Does he get angry when those who may be wiser disagree or suggest an alternative point of view?
Does he ever forgive those with whom he was angry?

2. How does he behave during a crisis?

Does he blame everyone except himself?
Does he become hostile towards an uninvolved member of an ethnic group that is known to abuse followers of Islam?
What steps does he take to face and deal with pressure?
Does he remain optimistic that things will get better, and that after every difficulty comes ease?

---

[1] *Islamic Sisters International*, vol. 3, no. 2, August-October 1994, Pp. 11, 29.

3. How does he feel about women's rights in a Muslim home?

Did he ever observe abuse from his father towards his mother?
Did he ever act or prevent abuse at home? How?
Does he believe that all women deserve abuse?
How does he make decisions? Does he rely on his own wisdom?
Does he consult with close friends?
Will he be willing to consult with his spouse on any decision?
Does he stick firmly to his decisions?

4. How does he deal with money matters?

Does he save money for the future?
Does he give money to charities?
When he decides to buy something, will he consult his spouse in
   making the decision?
How does he describe his own spending and attitude towards
   money?

5. What does he expect from his wife and children?

How would he react if his expectations are not met?
What is his vision of family life?
Would he pitch in and co-operate in family chores and the
   upbringing of children?
Would he be willing to change to accommodate your views?

6. What are his family like?

Are his family religious, or will you be the only one in hijab?
Does their approach to Islam differ from yours; will you be the
   only committed Muslims in a family whose Islam is more
   'traditional'?
If this is a mixed match, are his folks open to outsiders, or will
   you face clannishness and exclusion?

7. <u>What is his medical background?</u> (Many Imams in the US are now refusing to conduct marriage contracts until they see proof that the couple have undergone blood tests and been given a clean bill of health)

Has he ever had an AIDS test, and what was the result?
Is there any history of major illness in his family?

8. <u>What are his views on education of women and children?</u>

Will he allow you to continue and/or return to education?
What are his views on education and schooling of children? If you have strong views on Islamic schools, home-schooling, and so forth, find out if his view coincides with yours.
Will he take part in the children's upbringing and education? Will he teach them Qur'an?

9. <u>Where does he want to live?</u>

Does he want to settle in the country where you now live?
Does he want to return to his homeland? Does he want to move to a new country altogether?
Will the family have to move frequently because of his profession?
Will he take your feelings into account when deciding where to live?
Does he aspire to a large and luxurious home, or will he settle for less?
Does he want to live in the heart of the city, in the suburbs, or in an isolated rural setting?

Day-to-day matters

Some of these are individual preferences — what may deeply concern some may not even be an issue to others, but if you have strong feelings on a matter, it is better to get it out in the open before you make a commitment:

1. Food

Do you agree on the 'halal meat' issue? Some people will only eat halal-slaughtered meat, whilst others will eat any 'meat of the Jews and Christians' as long as it is not pork.
Does he insist on only eating the food of his own ethnic group, or are his tastes more eclectic?
Will he insist on having every meal cooked from scratch, or will you be able to have convenience food or take-away on busy days?
Does he have strong preferences for meat, or will you 'go vegetarian' some days?

2. Smoking

Does he smoke?
Do any of his family or friends smoke?
Will he let people smoke in your non-smoking home?

3. Going out

How does he feel about women going outside the home? Studying outside? Working outside?
Will he want to 'check out' your friends and only let you visit those of whom he approves?
How does he feel about women driving?

4. Pets

Are either of you keen to keep pets at home?
Do either of you have any allergies, dislikes or phobias when it comes to animals?

APPENDIX TWO

Islamic organizations
dealing with education

UK

Muslim Educational Trust
130 Stroud Green Road
London N4
UK   Tel. (0171) 2728502
Web site: www.muslim-ed-trust.org.uk

The M.E.T. is a well-established organization whose activities including sending Islamic studies teachers into state-run schools, organizing supplementary education, and publishing books and teaching aids on Islam.

CANADA

M.E.N.T.O.R.S. (Muslim Educational Network, Training and Outreach Services)
104-1920 Ellesmere Road., Suite 160
Scarborough
Ontario
CANADA M1H 3G1
Web site: www.mentorscanada.com

MENTORS is a community organization that works closely with the Toronto District School Board. Projects include home-schooling support, after-school tutoring for Muslim students, orientation sessions for public school staff and provision of resources and speakers on Islam. MENTORS also trains community support workers to liaise between Muslim parents and schools when necessary.

USA

Islamic Society of North America (I.S.N.A.)
P O Box 38
Plainfield
Indiana 46168
Tel: (317) 839 8157; (317) 838 8127
Web site: www.isna.net/Programs/pages/Programs.aspx

ISNA's Department of Program Development and Educational Services "plays an influential role in helping Islamic schools improve their curricula, find good staff members, and administer their schools more efficiently".

AUSTRALIA

Muslim Home Education Network Australia
(Based in New South Wales)
Web site: www.muslimhomeschool.net

Provides support and resources (including curricula) for home-schooling families.

The organizations listed above are just a small but important sample. There are many other excellent resources available to Muslim parents, in many countries, now accessible via the Internet on the Worldwide Web.

Glossary of Islamic terms*

'awrah   عورة   the part of a person's body that must be screened from public view; for males it is the area between the navel and the knees, and for females it is everything except the hands and the face

da'wah   دعوة   disseminating the teachings of Islam and calling people to accept and embrace Islam

Eid ('eed)   عيد   lit. festival; the two celebrations: one at the end of Ramadan and the other at the culmination of the Hajj

fajr   الفجر   dawn; the obligatory prayer at that time

fatwa (fatwah)   فتوة   religious decision or decree

ghusl   غسل   ritual shower necessary after a major impurity, e.g., after sexual intercourse or at the end of the menstrual period

Hadith (ḥadeeth)   حديث   the collected sayings and actions of Prophet Muhammad (ﷺ) that with the Qur'an form the basis of Islamic law

hadith (ḥadeeth)   حديث   a saying or action of Prophet

---

* The Arabic words are transliterated according to the conventions of the Transliteration Chart found in this book. If a word has become part of the English language (i.e., is found in a dictionary of Standard English), that spelling is used in this book and appears first in this Glossary, with the transliterated form in brackets after it.

		Muhammad (ﷺ) that was remembered and recorded by his Companions and followers
halal (ḥalâl)	حلال	permitted according to Islamic law
ḥarâm	حرام	forbidden according to Islamic law
hijab (ḥijâb)	حجاب	veil ordained by Allah for Muslim women
ifṭâr	إفطار	the meal eaten at sunset to break the fast
ijâzah	إجازة	*lit.* 'permission'; certificate issued to a scholar which qualifies him/her to teach what s/he has learned from his/her teachers or 'shaykhs'
inshâ' Allâh	إنشاء الله	God willing
'ishâ'	عشاء	evening; the obligatory prayer at that time
jazâkum Allah khayr	جزاكم الله خير	may Allah reward you with goodness
juz' (pl. ajzâ')	جزء	a section of the Qur'an equal to one thirtieth of the text
maghrib	مغرب	sunset; the obligatory prayer at that time
maḥram	محرم	a degree of consanguinity precluding marriage; a man whom a woman may never marry due to the close blood or marriage relationship, e.g., father, brother, son, uncle, and father-in-law
minbar	منبر	raised pulpit in a mosque from which the sermons are presented
muṣ-ḥaf	مصحف	copy of the Arabic text of the Qur'an that is neither accompanied by commentary nor translated

Ramadan (*Ramaḍân*)	رمضان	the ninth month in the Islamic calendar; the month of obligatory fasting
shaykh	شيخ	teacher, mentor, scholar
saḥoor	سحور	the pre-dawn meal eaten before the start of a fasting day
Sunnah	سنَّة	the practice and collected sayings of Prophet Muhammad (ﷺ) that together with the Qur'an forms the basis of Islamic law
takbeerât	تكبيرات	the act of repeatedly saying, *Allâhu akbar*, and other phrases praising Allah
taqwâ	التقوى	fearful awareness of Allah; being mindful of Allah; pious dedication; being careful not to transgress the bounds set by Allah
tarâweeḥ	تراويح	special communal night prayers performed only in Ramadan
Ummah	أُمَة	community or nation: *usu.* used to refer to the entire global community of Muslims
'umrah	عمرة	a minor, non-obligatory pilgrimage to Makkah
wuḍoo'	وضوء	ablution required before prayer or touching the Qur'an